Chicago White Sox 2020

A Baseball Companion

Edited by R.J. Anderson, Craig Goldstein and Bret Sayre

Baseball Prospectus

Craig Brown, Steven Goldman and David Pease, Consultant Editors
Robert Au, Harry Pavlidis and Amy Pircher, Statistics Editors

Copyright © 2020 by DIY Baseball, LLC.
All rights reserved

This book or any part thereof may not be reproduced or transmitted in any form or by any means, electronic or mechanical, including photocopying, recording, or by any information storage and retrieval system, without permission in writing from the publisher.

Limit of Liability/Disclaimer of Warranty: While the publisher and the author have used their best efforts in preparing this book, they make no representations or warranties with respect to the accuracy or completeness of the contents of this book and specifically disclaim any implied warranties of merchantability or fitness for a particular purpose. No warranty may be created or extended by sales representatives or written sales materials. The advice and strategies contained herein may not be suitable for your situation. You should consult with a professional where appropriate. Neither the publisher nor the author shall be liable for any loss of profit or any other commercial damages, including but not limited to special, incidental, consequential, or other damages.

Library of Congress Cataloging-in-Publication Data:
paperback
ISBN-13: 978-1-949332-68-1

Project Credits
Cover Design: Michael Byzewski at Aesthetic Apparatus
Interior Design and Production: Jeff Pease, Dave Pease
Layout: Jeff Pease, Dave Pease

Baseball icon courtesy of Uberux, from https://www.shareicon.net/author/uberux

Ballpark diagram courtesy of Lou Spirito/THIRTY81 Project, https://thirty81project.com/

Manufactured in the United States of America
10 9 8 7 6 5 4 3 2 1

Table of Contents

Statistical Introduction v

Part 1: Team Analysis

Chicago White Sox: Where Are You Going, Where Have You Been? 3
   Craig Goldstein, Nick Schafer and Matthew Trueblood

Performance Graphs 9

2019 Team Performance 10

2020 Team Projections 11

Team Personnel 12

Guaranteed Rate Field Stats 13

White Sox Team Analysis 15

Part 2: Player Analysis

White Sox Player Analysis 20

White Sox Prospects 103

Part 3: Featured Articles

The Baseball Is Juiced (Again) 119
   Robert Arthur

The Moral Hazard of Playing It Safe 123
   Craig Goldstein

Index of Names 129

Statistical Introduction

Sports are, fundamentally, a blend of athletic endeavor and storytelling. Baseball, like any other sport, tells its stories in so many ways: in the arc of a game from the stands or a season from the box scores, in photos, or even in numbers. At Baseball Prospectus, we understand that statistics don't replace observation or any of baseball's stories, but complement everything else that makes the game so much fun.

What stats help us with is with patterns and precision, variance and value. This book can help you learn things you may not see from watching a game or hundred, whether it's the path of a career over time or the breadth of the entire MLB. We'd also never ask you to choose between our numbers and the experience of viewing a game from the cheap seats or the comfort of your home; our publication combines running the numbers with observations and wisdom from some of the brightest minds we can find. But if you *do* want to learn more about the numbers beyond what's on the backs of player jerseys, let us help explain.

Offense

We've revised our methodology for determining batting value. Long-time readers of the book will notice that we've retired True Average in favor of a new metric: Deserved Runs Created Plus (DRC+). Developed by Jonathan Judge and our stats team, this statistic measures everything a player does at the plate–reaching base, hitting for power, making outs, and moving runners over–and puts it on a scale where 100 equals league-average performance. A DRC+ of 150 is terrific, a DRC+ of 100 is average and a DRC+ of 75 means you better be an excellent defender.

DRC+ also does a better job than any of our previous metrics in taking contextual factors into account. The model adjusts for how the park affects performance, but also for things like the talent of the opposing pitcher, value of different types of batted-ball events, league, temperature and other factors. It's able to describe a player's expected offensive contribution than any other statistic we've found over the years, and also does a better job of predicting future performance as well.

There's a lot more to DRC+'s story, and you can read all about it in greater depth near the end of this book.

The other aspect of run-scoring is baserunning, which we quantify using Baserunning Runs. BRR not only records the value of stolen bases (or getting caught in the act), but also accounts for all the stuff that doesn't show up on the back of a baseball card: a runner's ability to go first to third on a single, or advance on a fly ball.

Defense

Where offensive value is *relatively* easy to identify and understand, defensive value is...not. Over the past dozen years, the sabermetric community has focused mostly on stats based on zone data: a real-live human person records the type of batted ball and estimated landing location, and models are created that give expected outs. From there, you can compare fielders' actual outs to those expected ones. Simple, right?

Unfortunately, zone data has two major issues. First, zone data is recorded by commercial data providers who keep the raw data private unless you pay for it. (All the statistics we build in this book and on our website use public data as inputs.) That hurts our ability to test assumptions or duplicate results. Second, over the years it has become apparent that there's quite a bit of "noise" in zone-based fielding analysis. Sometimes the conclusions drawn from zone data don't hold up to scrutiny, and sometimes the different data provided by different providers don't look anything alike, giving wildly different results. Sometimes the hard-working professional stringers or scorers might unknowingly inflict unconscious bias into the mix: for example good fielders will often be credited with more expected outs despite the data, and ballparks with high press boxes tend to score more line drives than ones with a lower press box.

Enter our Fielding Runs Above Average (FRAA). For most positions, FRAA is built from play-by-play data, which allows us to avoid the subjectivity found in many other fielding metrics. The idea is this: count how many fielding plays are made by a given player and compare that to expected plays for an average fielder at their position (based on pitcher ground ball tendencies and batter handedness). Then we adjust for park and base-out situations.

When it comes to catchers, our methodology is a little different thanks to the laundry list of responsibilities they're tasked with beyond just, well, catching and throwing the ball. By now you've probably heard about "framing" or the art of making umpires more likely to call balls outside the strike zone for strikes. To put this into one tidy number, we incorporate pitch tracking data (for the years it exists) and adjust for important factors like pitcher, umpire, batter and home-field advantage using a mixed-model approach. This grants us a number for how many strikes the catcher is personally adding to (or subtracting from) his pitchers' performance...which we then convert to runs added or lost using linear weights.

Framing is one of the biggest parts of determining catcher value, but we also take into account blocking balls from going past, whether a scorer deems it a passed ball or a wild pitch. We use a similar approach—one that really benefits from the pitch tracking data that tells us what ends up in the dirt and what doesn't. We also include a catcher's ability to prevent stolen bases and how well they field balls in play, and *finally* we come up with our FRAA for catchers.

Pitching

Both pitching and fielding make up the half of baseball that isn't run scoring: run prevention. Separating pitching from fielding is a tough task, and most recent pitching analysis has branched off from Voros McCracken's famous (and controversial) statement, "There is little if any difference among major-league pitchers in their ability to prevent hits on balls hit in the field of play." The research of the analytic community has validated this to some extent, and there are a host of "defense-independent" pitching measures that have been developed to try and extract the effect of the defense behind a hurler from the pitcher's work.

Our solution to this quandary is Deserved Run Average (DRA), our core pitching metric. DRA looks like earned run average (ERA), the tried-and-true pitching stat you've seen on every baseball broadcast or box score from the past century, but it's very different. To start, DRA takes an event-by-event look at what the pitchers does, and adjusts the value of that event based on different environmental factors like park, batter, catcher, umpire, base-out situation, run differential, inning, defense, home field advantage, pitcher role and temperature. That mixed model gives us a pitcher's expected contribution, similar to what we do for our DRC+ model for hitters and FRAA model for catchers. (Oh, and we also consider the pitcher's effect on basestealing and on balls getting past the catcher.)

It's important to note that DRA is set to the scale of runs allowed per nine innings (RA9) instead of ERA, which makes DRA's scale slightly higher than ERA's. The reason for this is because ERA tends to overrate three types of pitchers:

1. Pitchers who play in parks where scorers hand out more errors. Official scorers differ significantly in the frequency at which they assign errors to fielders.
2. Ground-ball pitchers, because a substantial proportion of errors occur on groundballs.
3. Pitchers who aren't very good. Better pitchers often allow fewer unearned runs than bad pitchers, because good pitchers tend to find ways to get out of jams.

Since the last time you picked up an edition of this book, we've also made a few minor changes to DRA to make it better. Recent research into "tunneling"—the act of throwing consecutive pitches that appear similar from a batter's point of view until after the swing decision point–data has given us a new contextual factor to account for in DRA: plate distance. This refers to the distance between successive pitches as they approach the plate, and while it has a smaller effect than factors like velocity or whiff rate, it still can help explain pitcher strikeout rate in our model.

New Pitching Metrics for 2020

We're including a few "new" pitching metrics in the book for the 2020 edition, though unlike last year, these numbers may be a little bit more familiar to those of you who have spent some time investigating baseball statistics.

Fastball Percentage

Our fastball percentage (FB%) statistic measures how frequently a pitcher throws a pitch classified as a "fastball," measured as a percentage of overall pitches thrown. We qualify three types of fastballs:

1. The traditional four-seam fastball;
2. The two-seam fastball or sinker;
3. "Hard cutters," which are pitches that have the movement profile of a cut fastball and are used as the pitcher's primary offering or in place of a more traditional fastball.

For example, a pitcher with a FB% of 67 throws any combination of these three pitches about two-thirds of the time.

Whiff Rate

Everybody loves a swing and a miss, and whiff rate (WHF) measures how frequently pitchers induce a swinging strike. To calculate WHF, we add up all the pitches thrown that ended with a swinging strike, then divide that number by a pitcher's total pitches thrown. Most often, high whiff rates correlate with high strikeout rates (and overall effective pitcher performance).

Called Strike Probability

Called Strike Probability (CSP) is a number that represents the likelihood that all of a pitcher's pitches will be called a strike while controlling for location, pitcher and batter handedness, umpire and count. Here's how it works: on each pitch, our model determines how many times (out of 100) that a similar pitch was called for a strike given those factors mentioned above, and when normalized for each batter's strike zone. Then we average the CSP for all pitches thrown by a pitcher in a season, and that gives us the yearly CSP percentage you see in the stats boxes.

As you might imagine, pitchers with a higher CSP are more likely to work in the zone, where pitchers with a lower CSP are likely locating their pitches outside the normal strike zone, for better or for worse.

Projections

Many of you aren't turning to this book just for a look at what a player has done, but for a look at what a player is going to do: the PECOTA projections. PECOTA, initially developed by Nate Silver (who has moved on to greater fame as a political analyst), consists of three parts:

1. Major-league equivalencies, which use minor-league statistics to project how a player will perform in the major leagues;
2. Baseline forecasts, which use weighted averages and regression to the mean to estimate a player's current true talent level; and
3. Aging curves, which uses the career paths of comparable players to estimate how a player's statistics are likely to change over time.

With all those important things covered, let's take a look at what's in the book this year.

Team Prospectus

Most of this book is composed of team chapters, with one for each of the 30 major-league franchises. On the first page of each chapter, you'll see a box that contains some of the key statistics for each team as well as a very inviting stadium diagram. (You can see an example of this for the Milwaukee Brewers on this very page!)

We start with the team name, their unadjusted 2019 win-loss record, and their divisional ranking. Beneath that are a host of other team statistics. **Pythag** presents an adjusted 2019 winning percentage, calculated by taking runs scored per game (**RS/G**) and runs allowed per game (**RA/G**) for the team, and running them through a version of Bill James' Pythagorean formula that was refined and improved by David Smyth and Brandon Heipp. (The formula is called "Pythagenpat," which is equally fun to type and to say.)

Next up is **DRC+**, described earlier, to indicate the overall hitting ability of the team either above or below league-average. Run prevention on the pitching side is covered by **DRA** (also mentioned earlier) and another metric: Fielding Independent Pitching (**FIP**), which calculates another ERA-like statistic based on strikeouts, walks, and home runs recorded. Defensive Efficiency Rating (**DER**) tells us the percentage of balls in play turned into outs for the team, and is a quick fielding shorthand that rounds out run prevention.

After that, we have several measures related to roster composition, as opposed to on-field performance. **B-Age** and **P-Age** tell us the average age of a team's batters and pitchers, respectively. **Salary** is the combined team payroll for all on-field players, and Doug Pappas' Marginal Dollars per Marginal Win (**M$/MW**) tells us how much money a team spent to earn production above replacement level.

Ending this batch of statistics is the number of disabled list days a team had over the season (**IL Days**) and the amount of salary paid to players on the disabled list (**$ on IL**); this final number is expressed as a percentage of total payroll.

Next to each of these stats, we've listed each team's MLB rank in that category from first to 30th. In this, first always indicates a positive outcome and 30th a negative outcome, except in the case of salary—first is highest.

After the franchise statistics, we share a few items about the team's home ballpark. There's the aforementioned diagram of the park's dimensions (including distances to the outfield wall), a graphic showing the height of the wall from the left-field pole to the right-field pole, and a table showing three-year park factors for the stadium. The park factors are displayed as indexes where 100 is average, 110 means that the park inflates the statistic in question by 10 percent, and 90 means that the park deflates the statistic in question by 10 percent.

On the second page of each team chapter, you'll find three graphs. The first is the **2019 Hit List Ranking**. This shows our Hit List Rank for the team on each day of the 2019 season and is intended to give you a picture of the ups and downs of the team's season. Hit List Rank measures overall team performance and drives the Hit List Power Rankings at the baseballprospectus.com website.

The second graph is **Committed Payroll** and helps you see how the team's payroll has compared to the MLB and divisional average payrolls over time. Payroll figures are current as of January 1, 2020; with so many free agents still unsigned as of this writing, the final 2020 figure will likely be significantly different for many teams. (In the meantime, you can always find the most current data at Baseball Prospectus' Cot's Baseball Contracts page.)

The third graph is **Farm System Ranking** and displays how the Baseball Prospectus prospect team has ranked the organization's farm system since 2007.

After the graphs, we have a **Personnel** section that lists many of the important decision-makers and upper-level field and operations staff members for the franchise, as well as any former Baseball Prospectus staff members who are currently part of the organization. (In very rare circumstances, someone might be on both lists!)

www.baseballprospectus.com

Juan Soto LF
Born: 10/25/98   Age: 21   Bats: L   Throws: L
Height: 6'1"   Weight: 185   Origin: International Free Agent, 2015

YEAR	TEAM	LVL	AGE	PA	R	2B	3B	HR	RBI	BB	K	SB	CS	AVG/OBP/SLG
2017	NAT	RK	18	27	3	1	1	0	4	2	1	0	0	.320/.370/.440
2017	HAG	A	18	96	15	5	0	3	14	10	8	1	2	.360/.427/.523
2018	HAG	A	19	74	12	5	3	5	24	14	13	2	0	.373/.486/.814
2018	POT	A+	19	73	17	3	1	7	18	11	8	0	1	.371/.466/.790
2018	HAR	AA	19	35	4	2	0	2	10	4	7	1	0	.323/.400/.581
2018	WAS	MLB	19	494	77	25	1	22	70	79	99	5	2	.292/.406/.517
2019	WAS	MLB	20	659	110	32	5	34	110	108	132	12	1	.282/.401/.548
2020	WAS	MLB	21	630	92	30	3	35	102	85	123	5	2	.284/.382/.543

Comparables: Ronald Acuña Jr., Mike Trout, Tony Conigliaro

YEAR	TEAM	LVL	AGE	PA	DRC+	VORP	BABIP	BRR	FRAA	WARP
2017	NAT	RK	18	27	135	1.5	.333	0.0	RF(9): -1.1	0.0
2017	HAG	A	18	96	181	8.0	.373	1.0	RF(19): -1.9, LF(2): -0.3	0.9
2018	HAG	A	19	74	222	14.5	.405	0.3	RF(14): 1.1, CF(2): 0.2	1.2
2018	POT	A+	19	73	260	15.4	.340	1.4	RF(14): 1.0, LF(1): 0.0	1.6
2018	HAR	AA	19	35	113	3.6	.364	0.0	LF(4): 0.6, RF(4): -0.5	0.1
2018	WAS	MLB	19	494	125	40.5	.338	-0.5	LF(114): 2.7	3.0
2019	WAS	MLB	20	659	136	49.0	.312	1.4	LF(150): -0.8	4.9
2020	WAS	MLB	21	630	133	43.6	.310	-0.1	LF 3	4.8

Position Players

After all that information and a thoughtful bylined essay covering each team, we present our player comments. These are also bylined, but due to frequent franchise shifts during the offseason, our bylines are more a rough guide than a perfect accounting of who wrote what.

Each player is listed with the major-league team that employed him as of early January 2020. If a player changed teams after that point via free agency, trade, or any other method, you'll be able to find them in the chapter for their previous squad.

As an example, take a look at the player comment for Nationals outfielder Juan Soto: the stat block that accompanies his written comment is at the top of this page. First we cover biographical information (age is as of June 30, 2020) before moving onto the stats themselves. Our statistic columns include standard identifying information like **YEAR**, **TEAM**, **LVL** (level of affiliated play) and **AGE** before getting into the numbers. Next, we provide raw, untranslated numbers like you might find on the back of your dad's baseball cards: **PA** (plate appearances), **R** (runs), **2B** (doubles), **3B** (triples), **HR** (home runs), **RBI** (runs batted in), **BB** (walks), **K** (strikeouts), **SB** (stolen bases) and **CS** (caught stealing).

Statistical Introduction - xi

Next, we have unadjusted "slash" statistics: **AVG** (batting average), **OBP** (on-base percentage) and **SLG** (slugging percentage). Following the slash line is **DRC+** (Deserved Runs Created Plus), which we described earlier as total offensive expected contribution compared to the league average.

One of our oldest active metrics, **VORP** (Value Over Replacement Player), considers offensive production, position and plate appearances. In essence, it is the number of runs contributed beyond what a replacement-level player at the same position would contribute if given the same percentage of team plate appearances. VORP does not consider the quality of a player's defense.

BABIP (batting average on balls in play) tells us how often a ball in play fell for a hit, and can help us identify whether a batter may have been lucky or not…but note that high BABIPs also tend to follow the great hitters of our time, as well as speedy singles hitters who put the ball on the ground.

The next item is **BRR** (Baserunning Runs), which covers all of a player's baserunning accomplishments including (but not limited to) swiped bags and failed attempts. Next is **FRAA** (Fielding Runs Above Average), which also includes the number of games previously played at each position noted in parentheses. Multi-position players have only their two most frequent positions listed here, but their total FRAA number reflects all positions played.

Our last column here is **WARP** (Wins Above Replacement Player). WARP estimates the total value of a player, which means for hitters it takes into account hitting runs above average (calculated using the DRC+ model), BRR and FRAA. Then, it makes an adjustment for positions played and gives the player a credit for plate appearances based upon the difference between "replacement level"—which is derived from the quality of players added to a team's roster after the start of the season–and the league average.

The final line just below the stats box is **PECOTA** data, which is discussed further in a following section.

Catchers

Catchers are a special breed, and thus they have earned their own separate box which displays some of the defensive metrics that we've built just for them. As an example, let's check out J.T. Realmuto.

The **YEAR** and **TEAM** columns match what you'd find in the other stat box. **P. COUNT** indicates the number of pitches thrown while the catcher was behind the plate, including swinging strikes, fouls and balls in play. **FRM RUNS** is the total run value the catcher provided (or cost) his team by influencing the umpire to call strikes where other catchers did not. **BLK RUNS** expresses the total run value above or below average for the catcher's ability to prevent wild pitches and passed balls. **THRW RUNS** is calculated using a similar model as the previous two statistics, and it measures a catcher's ability to throw out basestealers but also to dissuade them from testing his arm in the first place. It takes into account factors like the pitcher (including his delivery and pickoff move) and baserunner (who could be as fast as Billy Hamilton or as slow as Yonder Alonso). **TOT RUNS** is the sum of all of the previous three statistics.

Justin Verlander   RHP
Born: 02/20/83   Age: 37   Bats: R   Throws: R
Height: 6'5"   Weight: 225   Origin: Round 1, 2004 Draft (#2 overall)

YEAR	TEAM	LVL	AGE	W	L	SV	G	GS	IP	H	HR	BB/9	K/9	K	GB%	BABIP
2017	DET	MLB	34	10	8	0	28	28	172	153	23	3.5	9.2	176	34%	.283
2017	HOU	MLB	34	5	0	0	5	5	34	17	4	1.3	11.4	43	32%	.194
2018	HOU	MLB	35	16	9	0	34	34	214	156	28	1.6	12.2	290	31%	.272
2019	HOU	MLB	36	21	6	0	34	34	223	137	36	1.7	12.1	300	36%	.219
2020	HOU	MLB	37	15	6	0	29	29	184	138	28	2.3	12.1	248	35%	.274

Comparables: Zack Greinke, A.J. Burnett, Aníbal Sánchez

YEAR	TEAM	LVL	AGE	WHIP	ERA	DRA	WARP	MPH	FB%	WHF	CSP
2017	DET	MLB	34	1.28	3.82	4.03	3.0	97.7	58	11	47.8
2017	HOU	MLB	34	0.65	1.06	3.08	0.9	97.5	59.6	15.1	49.9
2018	HOU	MLB	35	0.90	2.52	2.33	7.3	97.5	61.2	16.2	51.6
2019	HOU	MLB	36	0.80	2.58	2.51	7.9	96.8	49.9	17.5	48.3
2020	HOU	MLB	37	1.01	2.75	2.95	5.3	95.8	54.6	15.1	48.2

Pitchers

Let's give our pitchers a turn, using 2019 AL Cy Young winner Justin Verlander as our example. Take a look at his stat block: the first line and the **YEAR**, **TEAM**, **LVL** and **AGE** columns are the same as in the position player example earlier.

Here too, we have a series of columns that display raw, unadjusted statistics compiled by the pitcher over the course of a season: **W** (wins), **L** (losses), **SV** (saves), **G** (games pitched), **GS** (games started), **IP** (innings pitched), **H** (hits allowed) and **HR** (home runs allowed). Next we have two statistics that are rates: **BB/9** (walks per nine innings) and **K/9** (strikeouts per nine innings), before returning to the unadjusted K (strikeouts).

Next up is **GB%** (ground ball percentage), which is the percentage of all batted balls that were hit on the ground, including both outs and hits. Remember, this is based on observational data and subject to human error, so please approach this with a healthy dose of skepticism.

BABIP (batting average on balls in play) is calculated using the same methodology as it is for position players, but it often tells us more about a pitcher than it does a hitter. With pitchers, a high BABIP is often due to poor defense or bad luck, and can often be an indicator of potential rebound, and a low BABIP may be cause to expect performance regression. (A typical league-average BABIP is close to .290-.300.)

The metrics **WHIP** (walks plus hits per inning pitched) and **ERA** (earned run average) are old standbys: WHIP measures walks and hits allowed on a per-inning basis, while ERA measures earned runs on a nine-inning basis. Neither of these stats are translated or adjusted.

DRA (Deserved Run Average) was described at length earlier, and measures how many runs the pitcher "deserved" to allow per nine innings. Please note that since we lack all the data points that would make for a "real" DRA for minor-league events, the DRA displayed for minor league partial-seasons is based off of different data. (That data is a modified version of our cFIP metric, which you can find more information about on our website.)

Just like with hitters, **WARP** (Wins Above Replacement Player) is a total value metric that puts pitchers of all stripes on the same scale as position players. We use DRA as the primary input for our calculation of WARP. You might notice that relief pitchers (due to their limited innings) may have a lower WARP than you were expecting or than you might see in other WARP-like metrics. WARP does not take leverage into account, just the actions a pitcher performs and the expected value of those actions...which ends up judging high-leverage relief pitchers differently than you might imagine given their prestige and market value.

MPH gives you the pitcher's 95th percentile velocity for the noted season, in order to give you an idea of what the *peak* fastball velocity a pitcher possesses. Since this comes from our pitch-tracking data, it is not publicly available for minor-league pitchers.

Finally, we display the three new pitching metrics we described earlier. **FB%** (fastball percentage) gives you the percentage of fastballs thrown out of all pitches. **WHF** (whiff rate) tells you the percentage of swinging strikes induced out of all pitches. **CSP** (called strike probability) expresses the likelihood of all pitches thrown to result in a called strike, after controlling for factors like handedness, umpire, pitch type, count and location.

PECOTA

All players have PECOTA projections for 2020, as well as a set of other numbers that describe the performance of comparable players according to PECOTA. All projections for 2020 are for the player at the date we went to press in early January and are projected into the league and park context as indicated by the team abbreviation. (Note that players at very low levels of the minors are too unpredictable to assess using these numbers.) All PECOTA projected statistics represent a player's projected major-league performance.

Below the projections are the player's three highest-scoring comparable players as determined by PECOTA. All comparables represent a snapshot of how the listed player was performing at the same age as the current player, so if a

23-year-old pitcher is compared to Bartolo Colón, he's actually being compared to a 23-year-old Colón, not the version that pitched for the Rangers in 2018, nor to Colón's career as a whole.

A few points about pitcher projections. First, we aren't yet projecting peak velocity, so that column will be blank in the PECOTA lines. Second, projecting DRA is trickier than evaluating past performance, because it is unclear how deserving each pitcher will be of his anticipated outcomes. However, we know that another DRA-related statistic–contextual FIP or cFIP-estimates future run scoring very well. So for PECOTA, the projected DRA figures you see are based on the past cFIPs generated by the pitcher and comparable players over time, along with the other factors described above.

Lineouts

In each chapter's Lineouts section, you'll find abbreviated text comments, as well as all the same information you'd find in our full player comments. The only difference is that we limit the stats boxes in this section to only including the 2019 information for each player.

Managers

After all those wonderful team chapters, we've got statistics for each big-league manager, all of whom are organized by alphabetical order. Here you'll find a block including an extraordinary amount of information collected from each manager's entire career. For more information on the acronyms and what they mean, please visit the Glossary at www.baseballprospectus.com.

There is one important metric that we'd like to call attention to, and you'll find it next to each manager's name: **wRM+** (weighted reliever management plus). Developed by Rob Arthur and Rian Watt, wRM+ investigates how good a manager is at using their best relievers during the moments of highest leverage, using both our proprietary DRA metric as well as Leverage Index. wRM+ is scaled to a league average of 100, and a wRM+ of 105 indicates that relievers were used approximately five percent "better" than average. On the other hand, a wRM+ of 95 would tell us the team used its relievers five percent "worse" than the average team.

While wRM+ does not have an extremely strong correlation with a manager, it is statistically significant; this means that a manager is not *entirely* responsible for a team's wRM+, but does have some effect on that number.

PECOTA Leaderboards

If you're familiar with PECOTA, then you'll have noticed that the projection system often appears bullish on players coming off a bad year and bearish on players coming off a good year. (This is because the system weights several previous seasons, not just the most recent one.) In addition, we publish the 50th

Chicago White Sox 2020

percentile projections for each player–which is smack in the middle of the range of projected production—which tends to mean PECOTA stat lines don't often have extreme results like 40 home runs or 250 strikeouts in a given season. In essence, PECOTA doesn't project very many extreme seasons.

At the end of the book, we've ranked the top players at each position based on their PECOTA projections. This might help you visualize just how a given player's projection compares to that of their peers, so that even if a dramatic stat line isn't projected, you can still imagine how they stack up against the rest of the league.

Part 1: Team Analysis

Chicago White Sox: Where Are You Going, Where Have You Been?

Craig Goldstein, Nick Schafer and Matthew Trueblood

2019: What Went Right

It doesn't really feel like it, but there were a lot of things that broke the right way for the South Siders in 2019. The ever-elusive breakout happened for not one, not two, but three White Sox all in the same season, with Lucas Giolito, Tim Anderson, and Yoán Moncada all living up to their considerable hype.

Giolito's breakout lends credence to the scout's axiom about seeing it once and knowing it's in there to be developed—no matter what "it" is. In this case "it" is talent, because while the production is ace-level, making those who evaluated him as an amateur look good, the packaging is all new. This isn't the fire-breathing, hammer-wielding berserker who appeared in the scouting reports, but rather a sophisticated agent on the mound, with a still-deadly—but refined—fastball, and a changeup that will devastate its audience like the ending of *The Usual Suspects*. He's more James Bond than John Wick, is what I'm trying to say.

Yes, yes, the fastball came back—up to 94, but that's a long way from the upper-90s of his halcyon days. He's making it work anyway: Giolito's 2.81 DRA was eighth-best in the majors and his 5.7 WARP ranked fifth in the American League. This was about as far as he could get from his worst pitcher in the league standing of 2018. Other positives in the pitching realm include Aaron Bummer overcoming his last name to be quite a good reliever and potential closing option in the future.

Moncada and Anderson formed a dynamic and productive left side of the infield, leading the team in WARP with 5.1 and 3.9, respectively. Along with José Abreu and Eloy Jiménez they were the team's only batters to exceed 100 DRC+. Moncada became more aggressive in the box, reducing the unusually high number of called strike threes he received, and settled in nicely at the hot corner on defense. Anderson's early season fireworks on the field didn't exactly abate, but they did temper—and his batting line is supported by a helium-huffing .396 BABIP. His career BABIP rests at .342, so this isn't entirely out of character, but some focus on increasing his paltry 2.9 percent walk rate heading into 2020 might mitigate some of the oncoming regression in BABIP. Jiménez closed strongly (.340/.383/.710 in 107 September plate appearances) to rescue what had been a very inconsistent and borderline-disappointing rookie campaign.

Leury García had a hot stretch and has been one of baseball's best baserunners per BRR, while Abreu didn't fully bottom out, either. Alex Colomé's 2.80 ERA justifies the trade cost of Omar Narváez, but the peripherals aren't nearly as kind. That covers everything good.

2019: What Went Wrong

What went wrong with the White Sox' 2019 season traces back to the offseason. For a team to experience all the breakouts detailed above to struggle as much as Chicago has speaks to the flotsam and jetsam with which the rest of the team is held together. Manny Machado was their big offseason target and while they offered him by far the largest contract in organizational history, that's more of a statement on their general stinginess than it is a statement on the competitiveness of the contract. Would Machado have made 2019 a winning season? Almost certainly not, and it is hard to say how his occupation of third base might have affected Moncada, but age-26 superstars aren't available often, and the remainder of his prime would have coincided nicely with the White Sox apparent window. Not getting that deal done cast a pall over the season before it even started.

Left field was occupied by Jiménez, who hasn't thus far displayed any signs that there is a significant developmental hurdle in place. To quote Herm Edwards: we can build on this. What one cannot build on, though, is the fetid, seeping pile of detritus that accounted for fields center and right in 2019. That isn't wholly fair (and, to be honest, is quite rude) to García. He was a useful player who showed some potential Enrique Hernández qualities as a super-sub who plays nearly every day. At -0.3 WARP, he didn't quite make it to replacement level. It is fair and also rude to Adam Engel, who generated negative WARP and a 65 DRC+ in 248 plate appearances It's also applicable to Ryan Cordell, who has notched 247 plate appearances en route to a 68 DRC+ and 0.0 WARP.

Some of this is just how it goes when you're a team that has been rebuilding and isn't ready to make the leap. It's helpful to know that Engel and Cordell aren't going to be guys you need to keep around, barring a Giolito-like rise from the ashes, but that doesn't make it any easier to stomach.

Garbage fire is an overused phrase these days, but let's put a match to all of that and set it ablaze because, people, we're about to talk about the White Sox Designated Hitters! Yonder Alonso, Welington Castillo, James McCann, Matt Skole, and AJ Reed…COME ON DOWWWWNNNNN! Those free agent signings and former prospects, plus Abreu, combined into some sort of Voltron of decay and failure to produce negative WARP out of the DH slot. These *hitters* combined to average .205/.285/.356. This is the worst Remember Some Guys-assed position I've ever had the displeasure to look upon.

Dylan Cease has been the pitching version of Jiménez—it's been fine. The flashes of promise remain. Reynaldo López has been one of the worst pitchers in baseball, but he showed some slight progress in the second half, with a 4.29 ERA since July 14. Why isn't this in the section above? Because there's still his 5.38 ERA/7.06 DRA over the course of the full season. The other foundational franchise arms (Michael Kopech, Carlos Rodón) were either on the shelf to open the year or found themselves there quickly, with Rodon not expected back until the second half of 2020. Every other pitcher is better not discussed. —*Craig Goldstein*

Prospect Outlook

There is still some premium talent at Charlotte and below, despite the graduations of Jiménez and Cease. Freak athlete **Luis Robert** finally had a full healthy year in the States and he performed to the tune of a composite .328/.376/.624 line with 32 homers and 36 steals across three levels. Rick Hahn's failure to call him up in September says much more about the White Sox than it does about his major league readiness; he crushed Triple-A and ranks as the sixth-best prospect in baseball on your 2020 top 101.

Second baseman **Nick Madrigal** joined Robert near the top of that list, appearing at no. 13. Last season saw the diminutive middle infielder strike out only 16 times while drawing 44 walks in 532 plate appearances, reflecting his absurd contact skills. He slugged a modest .414, perhaps confirming some of the fears about whether his approach and unusually small frame will ever generate enough power in the majors. He, too, had an argument to play on the South Side in September. The White Sox also popped Andrew Vaughn third overall in the 2019 draft. He could have enough hit, power and zone control to be an impact player despite being limited to first base.

Michael Kopech sat out 2019 after undergoing Tommy John surgery, but remains a potential frontline starting pitcher if his recovery goes smoothly. Barring further incident, he should be ready to go at the beginning of 2020. Virtually all of the "next up" mid-to-back-end starting pitching candidates were injured, **Dane Dunning**, **Jimmy Lambert** and **Spencer Adams** among them. **Alec Hansen** is a reliever now and he's not exactly thriving in the role. Dunning, at least, may be ready for major-league looks at some point next year.

The position players beneath the very top layer were crushed in 2019 as well. **Luis Alexander Basabe** broke his hamate and then scuffled all year, **Blake Rutherford** couldn't crack a .700 OPS in Double-A and is no longer playing center field, and **Micker Adolfo** got hurt again. **Luis González** appears to have cut his strikeouts by attacking early in the count, but has not hit for average, power or drawn enough walks. **Jake Burger** has repeatedly injured his ankles. **Zack Collins** has made some swing changes and may yet carve out a career as a solid platoon 1B/DH who can catch in an emergency, but it's doubtful he would benefit from more time in Charlotte.

Though the ongoing rebuild has brought in a number of prospects from outside the organization, the White Sox continue to whiff on drafting and developing at far too high a rate. They will likely have to make up the shortfall in free agency unless a lot of the negative trendlines on the above prospects turn around. —*Nick Schaefer*

2020 Outlook

The best rebuilding projects don't feature a smooth transition from the reloading phase to contending for a playoff spot. They explode in a fury of concurrent development and massive expenditures. That's what's happened on the South Side of Chicago over the last year. Anderson, Moncada, and Giolito provided a stronger foundation on which to build than anyone had previously thought they would. Jiménez and Cease became symbols of the rebuild reaching full bloom. That seemed to be the cue for which the Sox front office was waiting. Extending Abreu, even after he accepted the qualifying offer, set a tone of aggressiveness and intentionality. Signing Yasmani Grandal to the biggest free-agent deal in club history not only radically made over the existing lineup and provided an immediate boost to the team's sloppy run prevention but signaled the crossing of the Rubicon.

After that, Chicago had to continue in that bold course, and they did it. Dallas Keuchel is a perfect fit for Don Cooper, for the Chicago rotation and for the financial sweet spot the team is in at the moment. Signing him for three years didn't foreclose any options for when they need to extend young players or start paying arbitration awards to other starting hurlers in the medium-term future.

After those three moves, it felt like other things would be icing on the cake, but Hahn continued about his work like a baker prepping for a three-year-old's birthday. Nomar Mazara is a low-ceiling addition, but drastically raises the floor in right field, where the Sox were one of the worst teams in baseball last year. Edwin Encarnación gives the heart of their lineup the depth and sheer power they'll need to rival the Twins. Gio Gonzalez has reached a point in his career wherein he is systematically and perpetually underrated, and the White Sox were the ones to take advantage of that this winter. Signing Steve Cishek stabilized the setup segment of the bullpen, and signing top prospect Robert to a preemptive mega-extension allows the team to pencil him into their Opening Day lineup without weighing whether that's worth losing a year of club control.

Madrigal will be the starting second baseman sometime in the first half. Kopech is healthy, and because of the timing of his 2018 Tommy John surgery, there's little reason not to expect him to be a member of the starting rotation right away. Of the 17 most important roles on the roster, seven have turned over, and every one of those changes is clearly for the better. That's an explosive transformation. —*Matthew Trueblood*

Performance Graphs

2019 Hit List Ranking

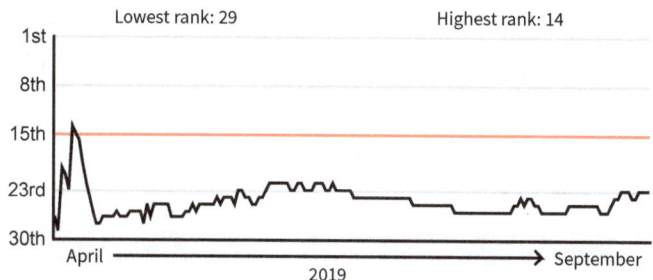

Committed Payroll (in millions)

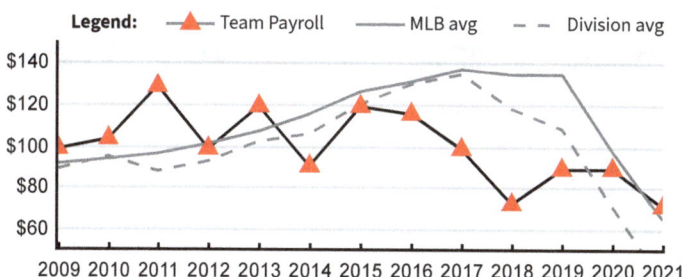

Farm System Ranking

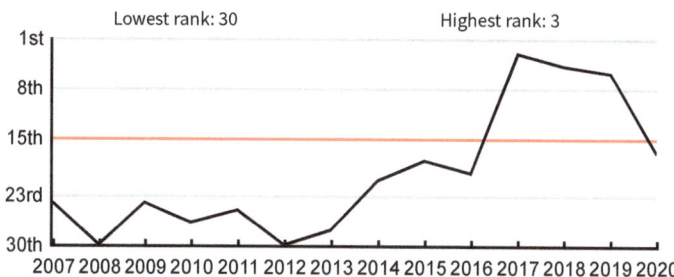

2019 Team Performance

ACTUAL STANDINGS

Team	W	L	Pct
MIN	101	61	0.623
CLE	93	69	0.574
CHA	**72**	**89**	**0.447**
KCA	59	103	0.364
DET	47	114	0.292

THIRD-ORDER STANDINGS

Team	W	L	Pct
MIN	97	65	0.597
CLE	87	75	0.535
CHA	**66**	**95**	**0.412**
KCA	59	103	0.364
DET	49	112	0.304

TOP HITTERS

Player	WARP
Yoán Moncada	5.1
Tim Anderson	3.9
Yolmer Sánchez	2.1

TOP PITCHERS

Player	WARP
Lucas Giolito	5.7
Aaron Bummer	1.7
Alex Colomé	0.9

VITAL STATISTICS

Statistic Name	Value	Rank
Pythagenpat	.423	24th
Runs Scored per Game	4.40	24th
Runs Allowed per Game	5.17	22nd
Deserved Runs Created Plus	89	25th
Deserved Run Average	5.77	27th
Fielding Independent Pitching	4.92	25th
Defensive Efficiency Rating	.698	21st
Batter Age	27.7	11th
Pitcher Age	27.5	8th
Salary	$88.9M	26th
Marginal $ per Marginal Win	$3.2M	21st
Injured List Days	1042	14th
$ on IL	14%	14th

2020 Team Projections

PROJECTED STANDINGS

Team	W	L	Pct	+/-
MIN	93.4	68.6	0.577	-8
CLE	86.1	75.9	0.531	-7
CHA	**82.5**	**79.5**	**0.509**	**10**
DET	69.2	92.8	0.427	22
KCA	67.8	94.2	0.419	9

TOP PROJECTED HITTERS

Player	WARP
Yasmani Grandal	5.9
Luis Robert	3.7
Eloy Jiménez	2.6

TOP PROJECTED PITCHERS

Player	WARP
Lucas Giolito	2.1
Dallas Keuchel	1.6
Alex Colomé	0.9

FARM SYSTEM REPORT

Top Prospect	Number of Top 101 Prospects
Luis Robert, #6	4

KEY DEDUCTIONS

Player	WARP
Yolmer Sánchez	0.2
Josh Osich	0.0
Welington Castillo	-0.1
Iván Nova	-0.7

KEY ADDITIONS

Player	WARP
Yasmani Grandal	5.9
Luis Robert	3.7
Edwin Encarnación	1.9
Yermin Mercedes	1.8
Dallas Keuchel	1.6
Nick Madrigal	1.0
Gio Gonzalez	0.7
Steve Cishek	0.2
Matt Foster	0.1
Adalberto Mejía	0.1

Team Personnel

Executive Vice President
Ken Williams

Senior Vice President/General Manager
Rick Hahn

Assistant General Manager
Jeremy Haber

Senior Director of Baseball Operations
Dan Fabian

Director of Player Development
Chris Getz

Manager
Rick Renteria

BP Alumni
Steffan Segui

Guaranteed Rate Field Stats

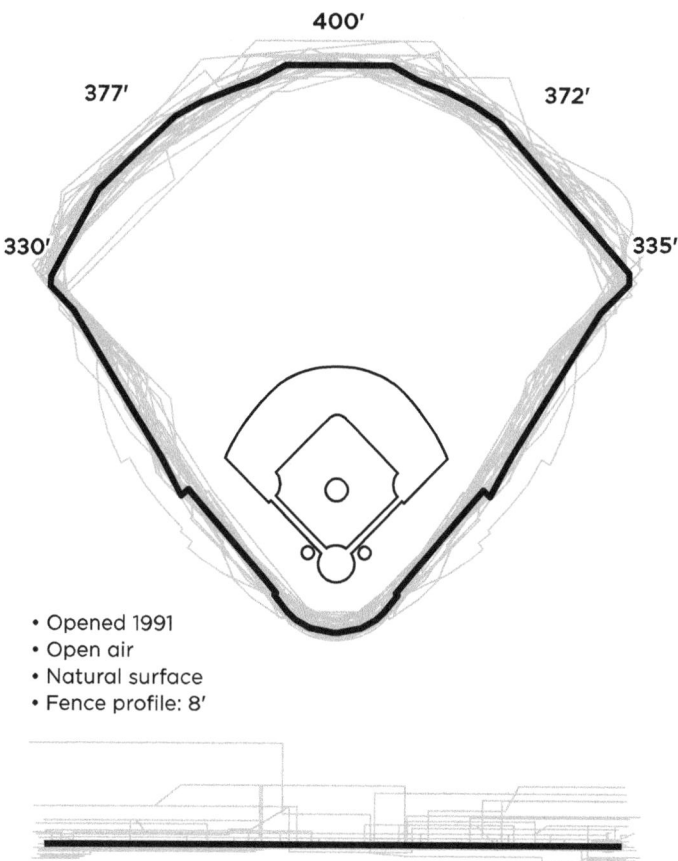

- Opened 1991
- Open air
- Natural surface
- Fence profile: 8'

Three-Year Park Factors

Runs	Runs/RH	Runs/LH	HR/RH	HR/LH
98	97	100	103	113

White Sox Team Analysis

Long before the creation of online tracking services, waiting for a package to arrive was an exercise of excitement and expectation. Your loving grandma would call and tell you she was shipping a package of delicious baked goods and that they would be delivered to your doorstep. She couldn't give an exact date, but she let you know it would be coming soon.

Over the last four years, White Sox general manager Rick Hahn has served as the fan base's grandma. Instead of promising cookies made with love, he would declare that better days were ahead—some that might even include playoff games. He couldn't give a precise timeline, either, of course, and at times he appeared more likely to kick the can down the road than deliver. But last season's progress and this past winter suggest Hahn is ready to make good on his pledge.

Unlike teams with plans of immediate contention, the success of the 2019 White Sox couldn't be measured in wins and losses. Rather, that club became defined by the development of their young, inexperienced players—players they hope will be part of their next playoff team. That was a good thing, too, considering the year started inauspiciously with failed pursuits of superstar free-agent hitters Bryce Harper and Manny Machado.

But the 2019 White Sox were able to salvage the year—and separate themselves from previous editions—by launching Lucas Giolito, Tim Anderson and Yoán Moncada to new heights. Add in Eloy Jiménez's introduction to the majors, and White Sox fans could hear the faint rumblings of a delivery truck.

It's rare for a player to catapult from average (or worse) production to being top-five at their position within a single season. Not only did the Sox have that happen once, but they had it happen with three different players. Giolito, Anderson and Moncada ended the 2018 season with a combined 1.1 Wins Above Replacement Player, a major disappointment for a team expecting growth from its cabal of formerly well-regarded prospects.

The most shocking of the three was Giolito, whose resurgence from a historically poor 2018 came with an adjustment to his arm action and his mindset. Always well-spoken and thought-provoking, the cerebral right-hander seemingly reached enlightenment after a winter of reflection and evolution. His confidence grew and that, combined with his shortened arm swing, allowed him early success and a sprouting presence on the mound. The pitcher who led MLB in both walks and earned runs the year prior was no more present than yesterday's breeze.

Chicago White Sox 2020

The White Sox have lacked a legitimate ace since Chris Sale was traded to the Red Sox in winter 2016. Giolito seems up for the task as serving as the face and anchor of a rotation with little experience but ample upside. The White Sox's only focus for Giolito should be ensuring he stays healthy enough to post the first 200-inning, 200-strikeout season of his career—a feat that could well enable him to rank higher than seventh in Cy Young Award voting.

For Anderson and Moncada, the adjustments were different, but just as effective.

Many hitting coaches would have tried to force Anderson into a box, getting him away from his natural strengths and free-swinging approach. The Sox took the scenic route, letting him grow and become a big-league hitter at his own pace. Their patience was rewarded in 2019, as he no longer wasted at-bats en route to the American League batting title.

Anderson won't have to repeat as champion to showcase his maturity in 2020. His ability to put the barrel on the ball has made him a dangerous hitter who is nearly impossible to retire within the zone. It's also allowed him to tap into his pop. Though Anderson is perhaps better known for his speed—he has swiped at least 15 bags in each of the past three years—power is part of his game. Were it not for an ankle injury that sidelined him for a month, he would've eclipsed both the 20-homer and 200-hit marks—making him the third White Sox hitter ever to do so.

As for Moncada, his breakout season began with an adjustment to his approach at the plate. The 24-year-old third baseman started attacking pitches earlier in counts, allowing him to cut down his strikeouts by six percentage points (from 33.4 percent in '18 to 27.5 percent in '19). His other results followed as he set career-highs in almost every notable offensive category.

Moncada has always had elite plate discipline, but it became more of a hindrance prior to last season as he would often take borderline pitches for strikes. Because of his increased aggressiveness, his walk rate dipped, falling to 7.2 percent. The drop in walks helped Moncada find his swing, but finding a new balance between that controlled aggressiveness and his superior eye at the plate took him from a good player to an elite player.

Should the gains stick, Moncada could lead the Sox in every offensive category in 2020. The question for Moncada is: how do you top a 5.7 WAR season?

Jiménez's arrival, meanwhile, should have brought a sparkle to the eye of White Sox fans. He produced in a big way, with an .828 OPS and a 105 DRC+. If not for a litany of freak injuries, Jiménez could have shown even more growth. Despite playing in just 122 games, he finished the season leading all American League rookies with 31 homers. Should he continue his ascend, he could live up to expectations of becoming one of the game's elite hitters over the next decade. (It doesn't hurt that he has star-caliber charisma, either.)

Soon enough, Jiménez and company will be joined by another phenom: Luis Robert. Robert captivated the baseball world in 2019, recording an impressive 30-30 season combined across three levels in his first full professional campaign. Not only is Robert's superstar potential undeniable; the opportunity to put him together with Jiménez for the next seven years should—at the very least—give the White Sox one of the most-formidable young duos in baseball.

In past years, this is the part of the White Sox essay where Nick Madrigal and Andrew Vaughn and other prospects would get name dropped and presented as the other great hopes for the club.

But unlike in those previous years, this time around Hahn added some legitimate outside help by signing one of the game's premier catchers, Yasmani Grandal, to give the White Sox a boost. Grandal is, in addition to being perhaps the best framing catcher in baseball, also a quality hitter no matter the position. Including 2019, he's posted a DRC+ over 100 in five of his six full-time seasons. For as good of a year as James McCann had, Grandal is a clear, substantive upgrade.

The White Sox, then, have the makings of a roster that is not only interesting, but brimming with the potential to end what has been a miserable 12-year period of baseball on the South Side. Still, there should be no pats on the back for Hahn and company until the wins come.

Since Hahn took over as general manager in 2013, the White Sox have the second-most losses in baseball (642), ahead of only the Miami Marlins (646). While high-end prospect acquisitions—like Jiménez, Moncada, Giolito, Reynaldo López and Dylan Cease—have contributed at the highest level, others—Micker Adolfo, Blake Rutherford, Jake Burger, Luis Alexander Basabe and Zack Burdi—have served as high-profile disappointments or busts. To add insult to injury, the White Sox have experienced a run of bad luck with pitchers needing Tommy John surgery. Five have undergone the knife in the last year, including Michael Kopech and Carlos Rodón.

Whether those development and injury woes are the result of bad luck or organizational deficiencies is impossible to suss out. What's certain is that turning around a franchise, from a rebuilding loser to a contending winner, takes more than a single successful offseason. It takes successful trades—for prospects and veterans; smart free-agent signings; continued player growth; and maintained health. All are easier said than done. Nevertheless, the White Sox will have to figure it all out—something they couldn't do during their previous years on the upswing, when they had Sale, José Quintana, Adam Eaton and others in town.

Will Hahn be up for the task? He better hope. The time has come when the word "rebuild," or any other cute synonyms non-competitive teams hide behind, should be removed from the White Sox's vocabulary. To sit at the big kids' table to get taken seriously requires acting the part. No more promises, no more lectures about the future or the importance of patience and flexibility. The White Sox have many of the pieces, now they need the wins.

Fortunately for fans, package tracking exists these days. And it looks an upgraded product—albeit not yet as delightful as grandma's cookies—will be delivered to the corner of 35th and Shields as soon as this season.

—Russell Dorsey is a Chicago reporter for MLB.com.

Part 2: Player Analysis

PLAYER COMMENTS WITH GRAPHS

José Abreu 1B
Born: 01/29/87   Age: 33   Bats: R   Throws: R
Height: 6'3"   Weight: 255   Origin: International Free Agent, 2013

YEAR	TEAM	LVL	AGE	PA	R	2B	3B	HR	RBI	BB	K	SB	CS	AVG/OBP/SLG
2017	CHA	MLB	30	675	95	43	6	33	102	35	119	3	0	.304/.354/.552
2018	CHA	MLB	31	553	68	36	1	22	78	37	109	2	0	.265/.325/.473
2019	CHA	MLB	32	693	85	38	1	33	123	36	152	2	2	.284/.330/.503
2020	CHA	MLB	33	595	74	31	1	28	86	36	135	2	1	.271/.329/.484

Comparables: Andres Galarraga, Michael Cuddyer, Mo Vaughn

Abreu is as strong as an ox and, especially in our current era of ball juiciness, capable of leaving the park just about any way he pleases. It's just that doing as he pleases, or as he feels he musts, is such an overriding principle in his plate approach that he will expand the zone frequently. Maybe if he could always step into a situation where the opposing pitcher felt the need to challenge him in the zone to stave off disaster, he would have something. With this in mind, Abreu will enter 2020 as the reigning American League RBI champion, thanks to him reserving all of his remaining vestiges of his 2014 form for the 190 plate appearances he strode up with runners in scoring position in 2019. It's a method, or at least a split, that he's repeatedly employed throughout his undeniably productive career, and might have even more success with as the White Sox offense expands beyond its previous setup of Abreu and eight guys until Abreu gets to hit again. But, as much as we always search for the loophole, the exception, the ingenious fix; he's still an aging right-handed first baseman, and he's getting steadily worse.

YEAR	TEAM	LVL	AGE	PA	DRC+	VORP	BABIP	BRR	FRAA	WARP
2017	CHA	MLB	30	675	130	34.1	.330	0.8	1B(139): 5.5	4.1
2018	CHA	MLB	31	553	114	14.7	.294	0.0	1B(114): 4.9	2.3
2019	CHA	MLB	32	693	108	18.0	.320	-5.1	1B(125): -10.5	0.2
2020	CHA	MLB	33	595	111	18.5	.313	-1.3	1B 0	1.9

José Abreu, continued

Batted Ball Distribution

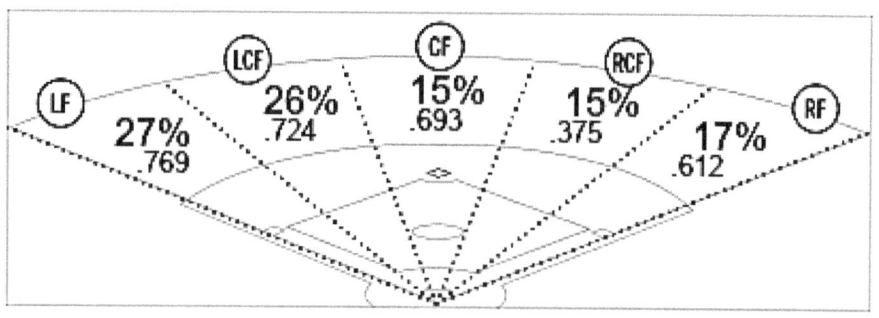

Strike Zone vs LHP   **Strike Zone vs RHP**

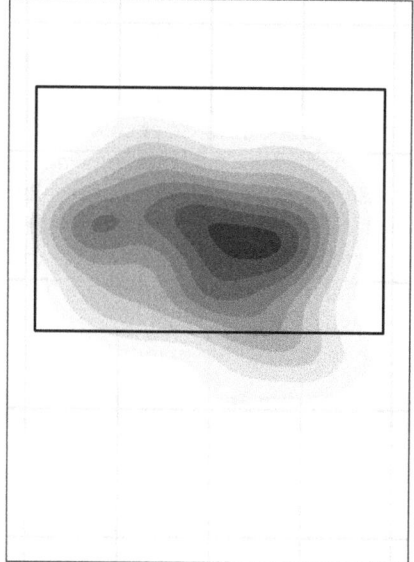

Chicago White Sox 2020

Tim Anderson SS

Born: 06/23/93   Age: 27   Bats: R   Throws: R
Height: 6'1"   Weight: 185   Origin: Round 1, 2013 Draft (#17 overall)

YEAR	TEAM	LVL	AGE	PA	R	2B	3B	HR	RBI	BB	K	SB	CS	AVG/OBP/SLG
2017	CHA	MLB	24	606	72	26	4	17	56	13	162	15	1	.257/.276/.402
2018	CHA	MLB	25	606	77	28	3	20	64	30	149	26	8	.240/.281/.406
2019	CHA	MLB	26	518	81	32	0	18	56	15	109	17	5	.335/.357/.508
2020	CHA	MLB	27	595	66	29	2	20	74	20	133	24	6	.284/.313/.447

Comparables: Billy Hunter, Chris Owings, Josh Rutledge

In 2018, Anderson and locker neighbor Daniel Palka posted identical .240 batting averages. In 2019, Palka batted .107, was optioned to the minors twice, and didn't launch his first home run until the final week of the season; Anderson batted .335, the highest qualified average of anyone in the majors. Casual observers will not struggle to conclude Palka, with his cartoonishly large leg kick and hand load and hyper-violent stroke, is even worse than a .240 hitter. Concluding that Anderson—a silky-smooth athlete with lightning-quick hands, a more upright stance than ever before and something bordering on a newfound compulsion to spray the ball to all fields—has radically improved is something we're all a bit more judicious about accepting. With two straight years of rangy but error-prone defense at short, consistent but average power and a lifelong aversion to walks, determining where he falls between a viable starting shortstop and a fringe All-Star is really just about his batting average—even in our statistically vibrant era. To that end, there were material improvements in contact rate and Anderson's ability to stay with and drive breaking pitches that will serve him well in years where he doesn't post the second-highest BABIP in the league. He just probably doesn't need to set aside space on his wall for more than one batting title plaque. (They do they get plaques, right?)

YEAR	TEAM	LVL	AGE	PA	DRC+	VORP	BABIP	BRR	FRAA	WARP
2017	CHA	MLB	24	606	78	11.1	.328	2.1	SS(145): -11.7	0.1
2018	CHA	MLB	25	606	92	19.5	.289	6.5	SS(151): 9.1	3.8
2019	CHA	MLB	26	518	113	33.8	.399	4.3	SS(122): 1.7	3.9
2020	CHA	MLB	27	595	98	24.3	.341	3.3	SS 0	2.5

Tim Anderson, continued

Batted Ball Distribution

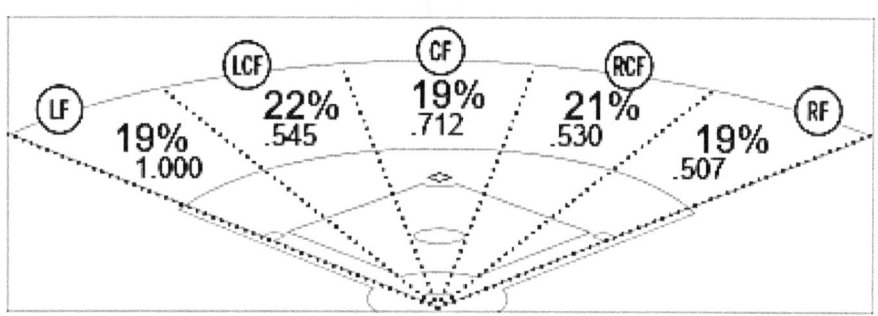

Strike Zone vs LHP   Strike Zone vs RHP

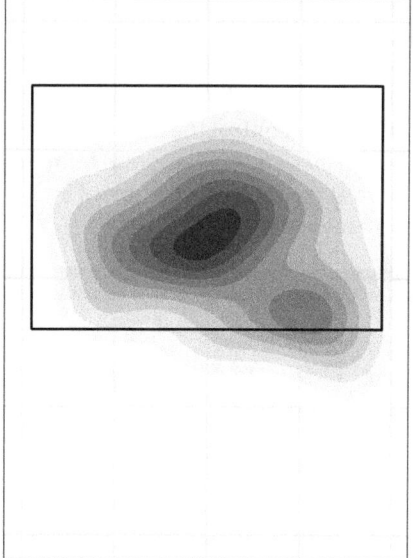

Chicago White Sox 2020

Zack Collins C

Born: 02/06/95 Age: 25 Bats: L Throws: R
Height: 6'3" Weight: 220 Origin: Round 1, 2016 Draft (#10 overall)

YEAR	TEAM	LVL	AGE	PA	R	2B	3B	HR	RBI	BB	K	SB	CS	AVG/OBP/SLG
2017	WNS	A+	22	426	63	18	3	17	48	76	118	0	2	.223/.365/.443
2017	BIR	AA	22	45	7	2	0	2	5	11	11	0	0	.235/.422/.471
2018	BIR	AA	23	531	58	24	1	15	68	101	158	5	0	.234/.382/.404
2019	CHR	AAA	24	367	56	19	1	19	74	62	98	0	0	.282/.403/.548
2019	CHA	MLB	24	102	10	3	1	3	12	14	39	0	0	.186/.307/.349
2020	CHA	MLB	25	140	16	6	0	6	17	19	48	0	0	.209/.320/.397

Comparables: Will Smith, Ryan O'Hearn, Derek Norris

With Collins off to a strong offensive start to 2019 in Triple-A, the White Sox gave him an early big-league cameo. It wasn't just a reward; they brought him up with the hopes that the Show would kick his butt and humble him into a new approach on both sides of the ball—especially offensively, where

YEAR	TEAM	P. COUNT	FRM RUNS	BLK RUNS	THRW RUNS	TOT RUNS
2017	BIR	1559	-1.8	-0.3	0.0	-2.5
2018	BIR	10814	-12.2	-0.9	-0.7	-14.5
2019	CHA	1653	-1.8	-1.1	0.0	-2.9
2019	CHR	6858	-3.9	-0.1	-0.3	-4.6
2020	CHA	1308	-1.0	-0.3	0.0	-1.3

he'd ideally control the zone rather than just punish mistakes. The Sox are touting incremental progress from Collins as evidence the 25-year-old will soon arrive at the final destination of an impact player. A reliable platoon DH is a more reasonable goal.

YEAR	TEAM	LVL	AGE	PA	DRC+	VORP	BABIP	BRR	FRAA	WARP
2017	WNS	A+	22	426	119	21.9	.282	-2.6	C(76): 1.5	2.4
2017	BIR	AA	22	45	164	4.7	.286	-0.1	C(11): -2.4	0.2
2018	BIR	AA	23	531	126	33.7	.329	-3.2	C(74): -14.4	1.5
2019	CHR	AAA	24	367	134	27.1	.346	0.8	C(50): -4.6, 1B(19): -1.6	2.1
2019	CHA	MLB	24	102	79	0.3	.295	0.0	C(10): -3.0, 1B(1): -0.1	-0.3
2020	CHA	MLB	25	140	89	1.0	.295	-0.3	1B -1, C -1	-0.1

Zack Collins, continued

Batted Ball Distribution

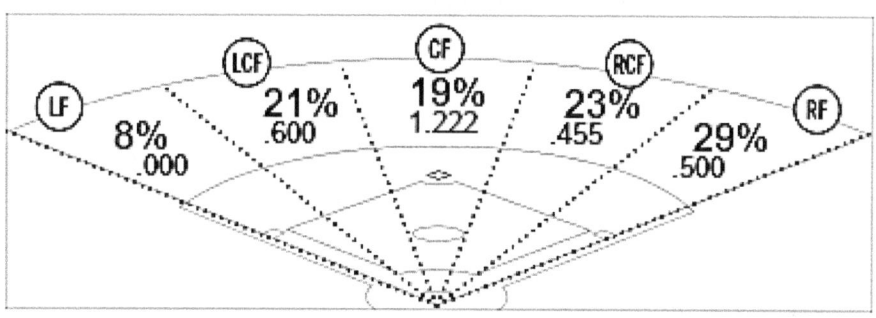

Strike Zone vs LHP **Strike Zone vs RHP**

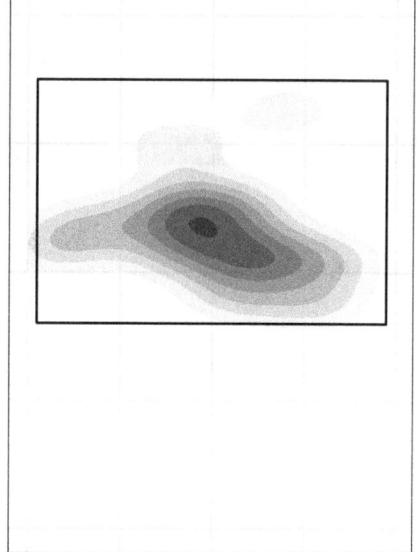

Chicago White Sox 2020

Cheslor Cuthbert CI

Born: 11/16/92 Age: 27 Bats: R Throws: R
Height: 6'1" Weight: 210 Origin: International Free Agent, 2009

YEAR	TEAM	LVL	AGE	PA	R	2B	3B	HR	RBI	BB	K	SB	CS	AVG/OBP/SLG
2017	OMA	AAA	24	68	10	3	1	4	9	7	11	0	0	.271/.353/.559
2017	KCA	MLB	24	153	10	7	0	2	18	9	39	0	0	.231/.275/.322
2018	KCA	MLB	25	117	11	2	0	3	7	11	23	0	1	.194/.282/.301
2019	OMA	AAA	26	219	25	17	1	8	35	17	46	0	0	.310/.370/.528
2019	KCA	MLB	26	330	24	14	0	9	40	19	67	1	0	.246/.294/.379
2020	CHA	MLB	27	251	25	12	1	7	28	17	55	1	0	.248/.304/.397

Comparables: Lonnie Chisenhall, Matt Dominguez, Brandon Drury

Sometimes prospects just stop being prospects without really becoming anything else. Cuthbert just kept playing baseball in 2019, without any real indication of what purpose it served; a utility infielder without utility who suffered through a 1-for-40 stretch in August. The thing is, thanks to injury and baseball's modern aversion to baseline competence, the one-time champion earned playing time in keeping with a full annual comment, and thus, we're compelled to keep writing. And writing. Reading this comment, in fact, is exactly what it feels like to watch Cuthbert play on a regular basis.

YEAR	TEAM	LVL	AGE	PA	DRC+	VORP	BABIP	BRR	FRAA	WARP
2017	OMA	AAA	24	68	109	4.7	.267	0.0	3B(10): 0.6, 1B(2): -0.2	0.3
2017	KCA	MLB	24	153	77	-1.5	.301	0.2	3B(44): 0.6, 1B(6): 0.0	0.1
2018	KCA	MLB	25	117	88	-3.7	.218	0.6	3B(12): 0.1, 1B(10): -0.9	0.1
2019	OMA	AAA	26	219	114	9.6	.366	0.9	1B(27): 0.0, 3B(9): -0.6	0.8
2019	KCA	MLB	26	330	82	1.2	.288	-1.7	1B(46): 0.2, 3B(40): -2.9	-0.3
2020	CHA	MLB	27	251	84	2.8	.297	-0.1	3B -1, 1B -1	0.1

Cheslor Cuthbert, continued

Batted Ball Distribution

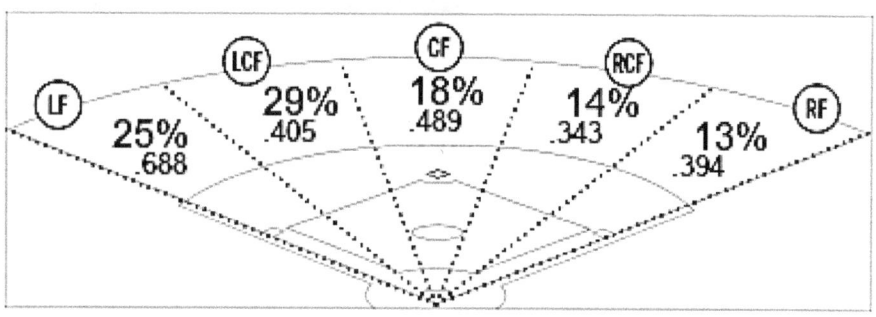

Strike Zone vs LHP **Strike Zone vs RHP**

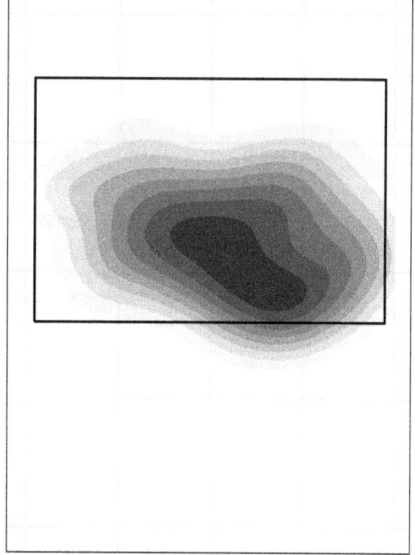

Chicago White Sox 2020

Edwin Encarnación DH
Born: 01/07/83 Age: 37 Bats: R Throws: R
Height: 6'1" Weight: 230 Origin: Round 9, 2000 Draft (#274 overall)

YEAR	TEAM	LVL	AGE	PA	R	2B	3B	HR	RBI	BB	K	SB	CS	AVG/OBP/SLG
2017	CLE	MLB	34	669	96	20	1	38	107	104	133	2	0	.258/.377/.504
2018	CLE	MLB	35	579	74	16	1	32	107	63	132	3	0	.246/.336/.474
2019	SEA	MLB	36	289	48	7	0	21	49	41	55	0	1	.241/.356/.531
2019	NYA	MLB	36	197	33	11	0	13	37	17	48	0	0	.249/.325/.531
2020	CHA	MLB	37	525	75	20	0	34	87	60	118	2	1	.241/.337/.509

Comparables: Jason Giambi, Eric Chavez, Albert Pujols

Everything about Encarnación aligned with the Yankees' team structure: A big bomber who's more of a designated hitter than a position player sporting an all-or-nothing approach. Though perhaps his biggest selling point at the trade deadline was acquiring him meant their divisional rivals, who were more in need of his thunder, could not. His veteran presence was welcomed on the young team, as were the stuffed parrots fans and teammates started displaying. But no matter how much excitement Encarnación's addition initially brought, his performance in the ALCS tarnished any positive impact he had in New York. His bat suddenly went ice cold and the parrot got a head start flying south for the winter, leaving Encarnación with just one hit in 18 at-bats while falling short to the Astros. The once-fun home-run race between him and Gary Sánchez earlier in the season turned into a strikeout race in the postseason. Encarnación still has a few more 30-homer seasons in him, something the White Sox are hoping to take advantage of in the short term.

YEAR	TEAM	LVL	AGE	PA	DRC+	VORP	BABIP	BRR	FRAA	WARP
2017	CLE	MLB	34	669	142	28.9	.271	-5.2	1B(23): -0.6	3.8
2018	CLE	MLB	35	579	125	12.4	.265	-5.1	1B(23): 0.8	2.1
2019	SEA	MLB	36	289	135	17.2	.220	0.6	1B(45): -0.6, 2B(1): 0.0	1.7
2019	NYA	MLB	36	197	128	10.6	.267	-1.7	1B(12): -0.4	0.8
2020	CHA	MLB	37	525	118	15.5	.250	-3.0	1B 0	1.6

Edwin Encarnación, continued

Batted Ball Distribution

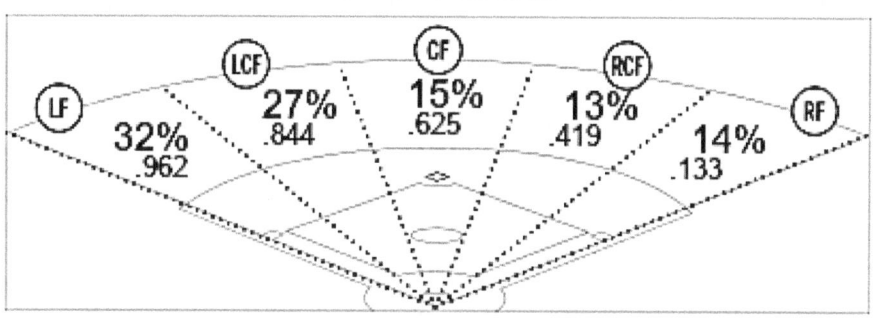

Strike Zone vs LHP   **Strike Zone vs RHP**

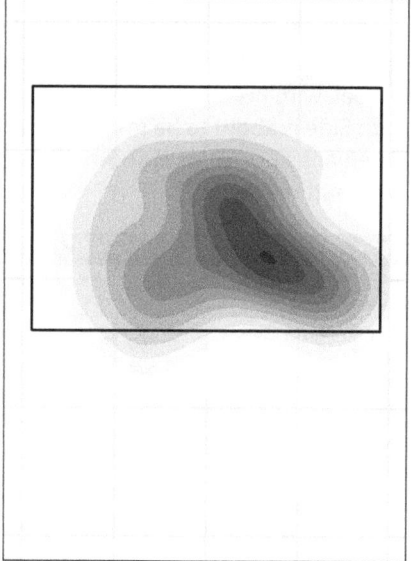

Adam Engel CF

Born: 12/09/91   Age: 28   Bats: R   Throws: R
Height: 6'2"   Weight: 210   Origin: Round 19, 2013 Draft (#573 overall)

YEAR	TEAM	LVL	AGE	PA	R	2B	3B	HR	RBI	BB	K	SB	CS	AVG/OBP/SLG
2017	CHR	AAA	25	192	20	12	2	8	19	19	51	4	3	.218/.312/.461
2017	CHA	MLB	25	336	34	11	3	6	21	19	117	8	1	.166/.235/.282
2018	CHA	MLB	26	463	49	17	4	6	29	18	129	16	8	.235/.279/.336
2019	CHR	AAA	27	277	43	13	4	9	29	22	62	13	3	.270/.347/.464
2019	CHA	MLB	27	248	26	10	2	6	26	14	78	3	3	.242/.304/.383
2020	CHA	MLB	28	210	20	8	1	5	21	13	65	10	3	.214/.277/.350

Comparables: Drew Stubbs, Jordan Danks, Aaron Hicks

In 2019, the White Sox seemed to have gotten fed up with Engel's brand of athletic and increasingly instinctual center-field defense paired with, at most, bimonthly outbursts of offensive impact. They optioned him to Triple-A in early May amid a wave of reassignments to try to jolt a struggling roster—and it sort of worked? Engel toiled in Charlotte for over two months, hit as well there as every single human being in that ballpark did in 2019 and returned to Chicago not, like, transformed or anything, but capable of running into the occasional meatball with his deceptive raw strength. The starting center fielder job on the South Side is about to be reserved for the next several years, which could be convenient since Engel is showing glimpses of being able to hit enough to be a fourth outfielder.

YEAR	TEAM	LVL	AGE	PA	DRC+	VORP	BABIP	BRR	FRAA	WARP
2017	CHR	AAA	25	192	92	10.0	.262	1.8	CF(33): -0.3, LF(13): 1.9	0.8
2017	CHA	MLB	25	336	46	-9.0	.247	1.4	CF(95): 7.9, LF(1): 0.0	-0.2
2018	CHA	MLB	26	463	68	-1.3	.322	1.5	CF(140): 10.0	1.0
2019	CHR	AAA	27	277	92	9.2	.328	4.0	CF(58): 7.4, LF(5): -0.4	1.6
2019	CHA	MLB	27	248	65	-2.1	.343	0.6	CF(86): 0.8	-0.1
2020	CHA	MLB	28	210	68	-0.4	.295	0.6	CF 4	0.3

Adam Engel, continued

Batted Ball Distribution

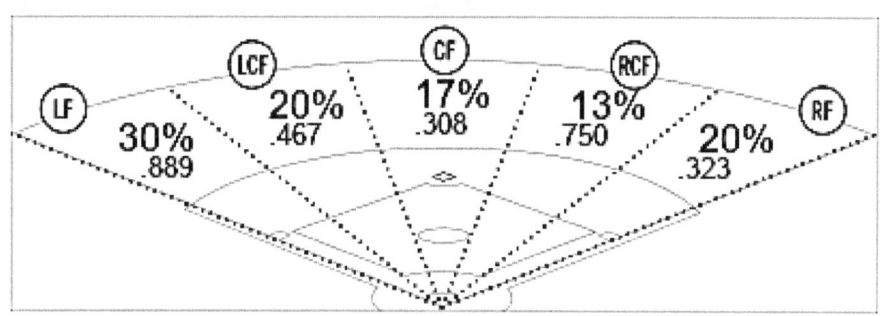

Strike Zone vs LHP   **Strike Zone vs RHP**

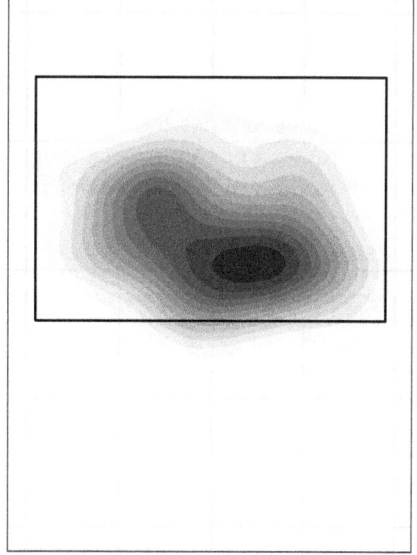

Leury García UT

Born: 03/18/91 Age: 29 Bats: B Throws: R
Height: 5'8" Weight: 180 Origin: International Free Agent, 2007

YEAR	TEAM	LVL	AGE	PA	R	2B	3B	HR	RBI	BB	K	SB	CS	AVG/OBP/SLG
2017	CHA	MLB	26	326	41	15	2	9	33	13	69	8	5	.270/.316/.423
2018	CHA	MLB	27	275	23	7	4	4	32	9	69	12	1	.271/.303/.376
2019	CHA	MLB	28	618	93	27	3	8	40	21	139	15	5	.279/.310/.378
2020	CHA	MLB	29	385	36	14	2	7	38	16	94	15	6	.255/.295/.366

Comparables: Jeff Bianchi, Charlie Culberson, George Kell

García was surprised when he was told two days prior to the game that he was going to be the White Sox Opening Day leadoff man and center fielder. One can only imagine what he would have thought of the idea seven years ago, when he was a glove-first shortstop. Not every avant garde idea is a great one. After two seasons shortened by nagging injuries, García finally showed he could navigate the travails of full-season play, but in doing that, strongly supported the conclusion that he's ideally a part-time player. His batting line crested at .301/.335/.405 after a four-hit night on Independence Day, and given what became of his second half, someone might consider cutting him off at exactly 327 plate appearances in 2020. García's helter-skelter approach produces a good average, but not good enough to counter the disparities everywhere else. He can run, but not quite fast enough to counter the lack of other weapons. He can play everywhere, but not well enough to be a net positive at somewhere specific. Four-hit nights like July 4 are in him, just don't come around asking for the same thing on July 5.

YEAR	TEAM	LVL	AGE	PA	DRC+	VORP	BABIP	BRR	FRAA	WARP
2017	CHA	MLB	26	326	82	7.5	.321	0.5	CF(51): 3.4, LF(24): 0.2	0.8
2018	CHA	MLB	27	275	74	4.9	.355	1.8	LF(40): 1.4, CF(26): -0.8	0.3
2019	CHA	MLB	28	618	78	3.6	.353	7.9	CF(80): -5.4, RF(45): -2.7	0.3
2020	CHA	MLB	29	385	76	2.5	.325	2.1	2B 1, RF -2	0.1

Leury García, continued

Batted Ball Distribution

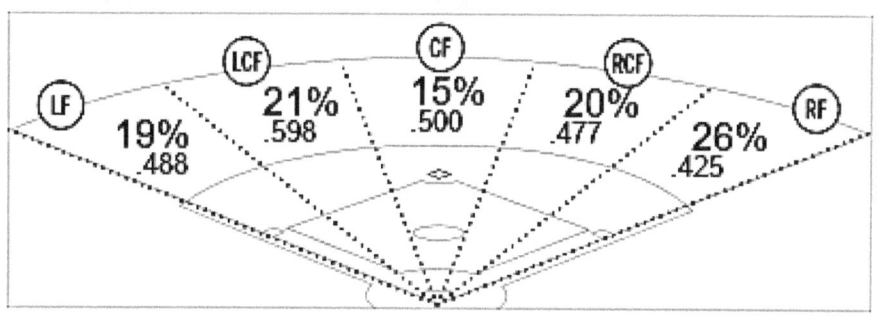

Strike Zone vs LHP　　　**Strike Zone vs RHP**

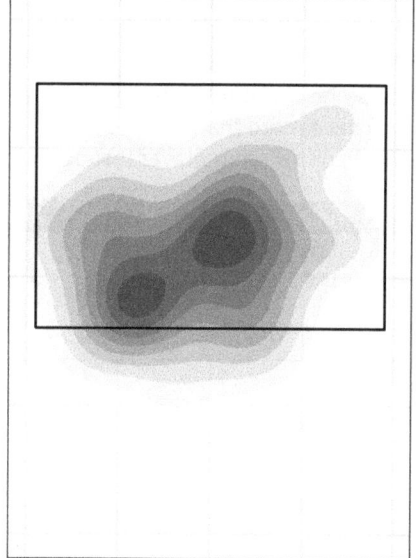

Yasmani Grandal C

Born: 11/08/88 Age: 31 Bats: B Throws: R
Height: 6'1" Weight: 235 Origin: Round 1, 2010 Draft (#12 overall)

YEAR	TEAM	LVL	AGE	PA	R	2B	3B	HR	RBI	BB	K	SB	CS	AVG/OBP/SLG
2017	LAN	MLB	28	482	50	27	0	22	58	40	130	0	1	.247/.308/.459
2018	LAN	MLB	29	518	65	23	2	24	68	72	124	2	1	.241/.349/.466
2019	MIL	MLB	30	632	79	26	2	28	77	109	139	5	1	.246/.380/.468
2020	CHA	MLB	31	560	76	21	1	28	81	88	131	3	1	.235/.359/.460

Comparables: Carlos Santana, Chris Iannetta, Duke Sims

YEAR	TEAM	P. COUNT	FRM RUNS	BLK RUNS	THRW RUNS	TOT RUNS
2017	LAN	16211	26.2	-1.4	1.3	26.2
2018	LAN	16615	15.7	0.8	0.1	16.3
2019	MIL	18727	19.4	1.8	-0.1	20.9
2020	CHA	21509	27.4	0.4	0.0	27.8

Grandal bet on himself the winter before last by foregoing at least one reported multi-year offer in favor of a one-year deal with the Brewers. After a fourth-straight 20-dinger season, Grandal's wager paid off as he signed a four-year deal worth $73 million with the White Sox. It was a smart signing on GM Rick Hahn's part, as there aren't many backstops who are elite framers in addition to being high-quality hitters—he was one of just four backstops in 2019 to slug better than .450 and reach base more than 35 percent of the time. Grandal has, for whatever reason, been an underrated player throughout his career. It's time for that to change.

YEAR	TEAM	LVL	AGE	PA	DRC+	VORP	BABIP	BRR	FRAA	WARP
2017	LAN	MLB	28	482	93	25.2	.298	-2.6	C(117): 27.7	4.5
2018	LAN	MLB	29	518	113	36.6	.278	-4.4	C(135): 17.7, 1B(2): 0.0	4.7
2019	MIL	MLB	30	632	124	50.1	.279	-7.5	C(137): 19.9, 1B(20): 0.2	6.1
2020	CHA	MLB	31	560	113	29.5	.266	-4.3	C 28, 1B 0	6.0

Yasmani Grandal, continued

Batted Ball Distribution

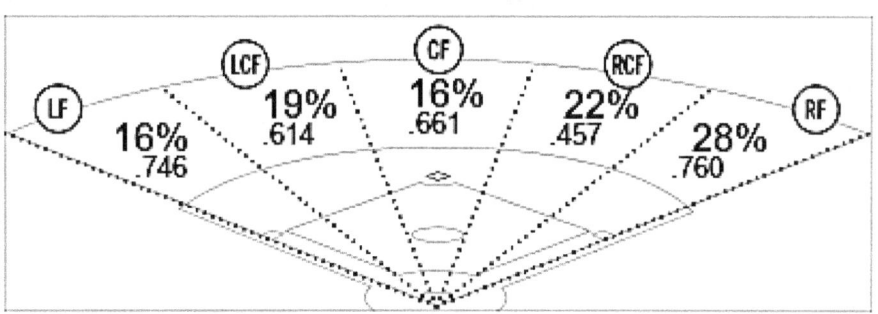

Strike Zone vs LHP   **Strike Zone vs RHP**

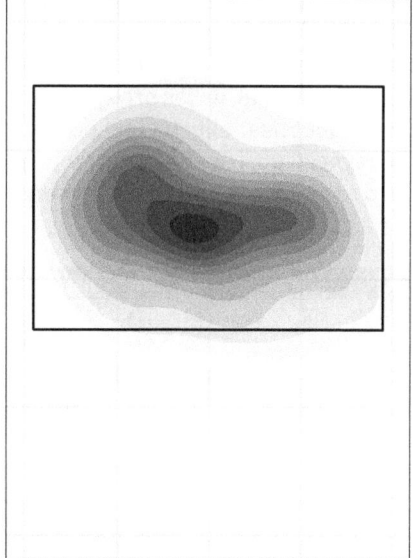

Eloy Jiménez LF

Born: 11/27/96   Age: 23   Bats: R   Throws: R
Height: 6'4"   Weight: 205   Origin: International Free Agent, 2013

YEAR	TEAM	LVL	AGE	PA	R	2B	3B	HR	RBI	BB	K	SB	CS	AVG/OBP/SLG
2017	MYR	A+	20	174	23	6	2	8	32	18	35	0	0	.271/.351/.490
2017	WNS	A+	20	122	20	11	1	8	26	12	21	0	2	.345/.410/.682
2017	BIR	AA	20	73	11	5	0	3	7	5	16	1	1	.353/.397/.559
2018	BIR	AA	21	228	36	15	2	10	42	18	39	0	0	.317/.368/.556
2018	CHR	AAA	21	228	28	13	1	12	33	14	30	0	1	.355/.399/.597
2019	CHA	MLB	22	504	69	18	2	31	79	30	134	0	0	.267/.315/.513
2020	CHA	MLB	23	595	80	25	1	37	98	34	155	1	1	.271/.316/.519

Comparables: Maikel Franco, Clint Frazier, Manuel Margot

Jiménez kind of stunk for much of a full rookie season (enabled by a late-spring contract extension to head off service-time games). He waved at sliders out of the zone, which were flung at him at the league's-highest rate. He flopped around and slammed into objects both stationary and in motion while playing left field—frequently at his own physical peril. And so on. For the baseball writing world, who declared Jiménez was big-league ready—eminently so—early in 2018, it was pretty awkward. Just imagine how Eloy felt! But the thing about near-elite hit and power tools working in concert, is that eventually they synced up, leaving him with respectable end-of-season numbers. He'll need to figure out how to play defense and how to stay healthy, but the bat is there.

YEAR	TEAM	LVL	AGE	PA	DRC+	VORP	BABIP	BRR	FRAA	WARP
2017	MYR	A+	20	174	158	9.5	.304	-0.3	LF(17): 0.3, RF(7): -0.1	2.0
2017	WNS	A+	20	122	158	13.6	.370	0.4	RF(21): -0.6	1.9
2017	BIR	AA	20	73	170	8.5	.429	0.1	RF(15): -1.1	0.5
2018	BIR	AA	21	228	161	23.9	.344	-1.3	LF(30): -3.6, RF(13): -1.8	1.2
2018	CHR	AAA	21	228	181	19.9	.371	-1.8	LF(41): -0.2, RF(6): 0.0	2.1
2019	CHA	MLB	22	504	105	17.1	.308	1.0	LF(114): -0.7	1.7
2020	CHA	MLB	23	595	114	27.2	.312	0.8	LF -1	2.7

Eloy Jiménez, continued

Batted Ball Distribution

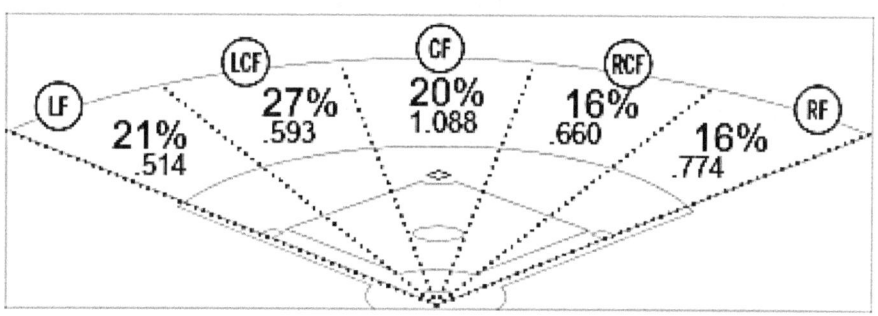

Strike Zone vs LHP **Strike Zone vs RHP**

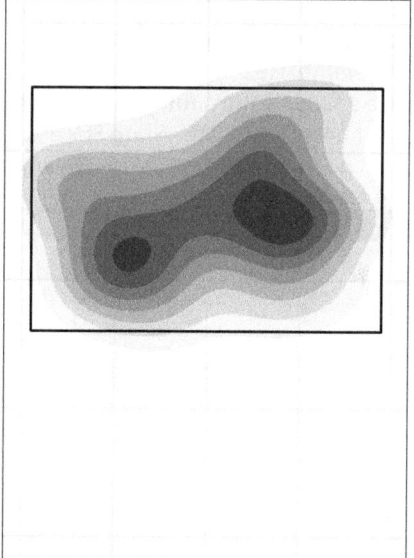

Chicago White Sox 2020

Nomar Mazara   RF
Born: 04/26/95   Age: 25   Bats: L   Throws: L
Height: 6'4"   Weight: 215   Origin: International Free Agent, 2011

YEAR	TEAM	LVL	AGE	PA	R	2B	3B	HR	RBI	BB	K	SB	CS	AVG/OBP/SLG
2017	TEX	MLB	22	616	64	30	2	20	101	55	127	2	2	.253/.323/.422
2018	TEX	MLB	23	536	61	25	1	20	77	40	116	1	0	.258/.317/.436
2019	TEX	MLB	24	469	69	27	1	19	66	28	108	4	1	.268/.318/.469
2020	CHA	MLB	25	455	54	20	1	20	62	33	103	1	1	.255/.315/.451

Comparables: Jeremy Hermida, Jose Tabata, Shawn Green

It's not exactly Khris Davis' penchant for hitting .247, but it should be fairly easy to project Mazara's offensive output for 2020. Mazara was pegged as a mega-prospect, so his numbers are obviously underwhelming thus far, but the consistency is truly amazing given how Mazara's proclivity towards streaks. Looking at Mazara's season-end numbers is like assessing a room containing only NBA centers and second-grade children and surmising that the average height of people in the room is 5-foot-10. Mazara is never a 5-foot-10 baseball player. He's either hitting monster home runs in bunches or mired in a month-long slump. He's still just 24 (he'll be 25 in April) so there's time yet for him to have a fully healthy, fully consistent season, but the Rangers have decided it won't be in Texas. The White Sox are simply hoping it happens at all, and paid a small price in prospect Steele Walker to find out.

YEAR	TEAM	LVL	AGE	PA	DRC+	VORP	BABIP	BRR	FRAA	WARP
2017	TEX	MLB	22	616	91	0.5	.293	-2.4	RF(92): -6.2, LF(47): 0.8	-0.1
2018	TEX	MLB	23	536	98	5.2	.298	-1.2	RF(113): -10.2, LF(2): -0.2	-0.2
2019	TEX	MLB	24	469	95	7.6	.312	-1.4	RF(101): -5.1	0.1
2020	CHA	MLB	25	455	98	7.5	.293	-1.2	RF -9	-0.1

Nomar Mazara, continued

Batted Ball Distribution

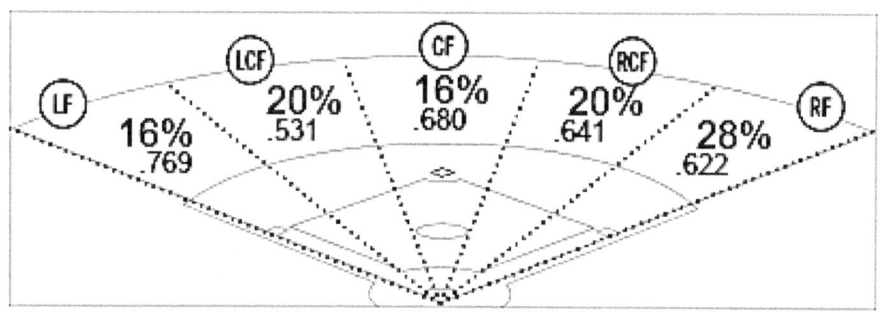

Strike Zone vs LHP

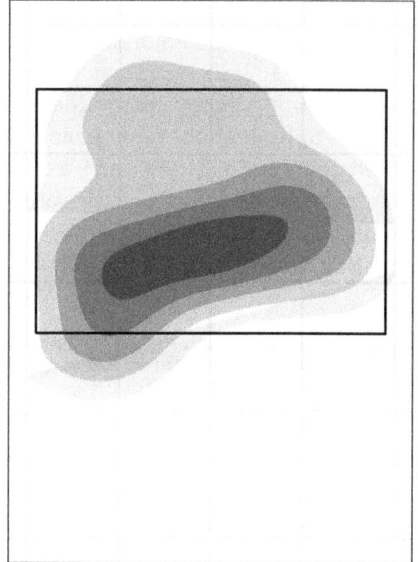

Strike Zone vs RHP

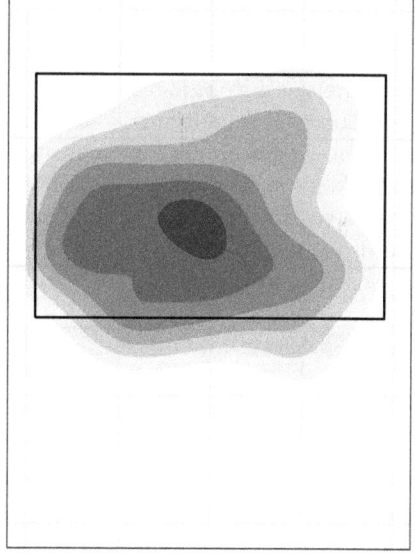

White Sox Player Analysis - 39

James McCann C

Born: 06/13/90 Age: 30 Bats: R Throws: R
Height: 6'3" Weight: 225 Origin: Round 2, 2011 Draft (#76 overall)

YEAR	TEAM	LVL	AGE	PA	R	2B	3B	HR	RBI	BB	K	SB	CS	AVG/OBP/SLG
2017	DET	MLB	27	391	39	14	2	13	49	26	89	1	0	.253/.318/.415
2018	DET	MLB	28	457	31	16	0	8	39	26	116	0	3	.220/.267/.314
2019	CHA	MLB	29	476	62	26	1	18	60	30	137	4	1	.273/.328/.460
2020	CHA	MLB	30	210	22	8	1	7	25	13	61	1	0	.242/.296/.405

Comparables: Gerald Laird, Chad Moeller, Austin Romine

Cutting loose their former second-round pick and longtime veteran backstop to save a couple million after a career-worst offensive year is not the reason the Tigers went from 98 losses to 114 in 2019. But it doesn't seem to have been a positive maneuver, either—not after McCann rode a magic carpet to a shocking All-Star appearance with the team five hours away while the Tigers got a .186/.234/.321 slash line from their backstops in his stead. To be fair, even during a good season there were some clear deficiencies with his game. He's upfront about valuing blocking and throwing over framing—a position backed up by our metrics—and his on-base skills are light, to say the least of it. Whatever can be said about the value of a personable and thoughtful game-caller and clubhouse chairman, those words wound up getting said about McCann. Now that he's hitting his weight again, there's reason to listen.

YEAR	TEAM	P. COUNT	FRM RUNS	BLK RUNS	THRW RUNS	TOT RUNS
2017	DET	14626	-13.2	-3.4	-0.8	-18.6
2018	DET	16526	-2.3	-1.4	1.1	-2.9
2019	CHA	15318	-8.0	-0.9	0.9	-7.6
2020	CHA	8154	-3.3	-0.3	0.6	-3.0

YEAR	TEAM	LVL	AGE	PA	DRC+	VORP	BABIP	BRR	FRAA	WARP
2017	DET	MLB	27	391	96	13.7	.300	-0.9	C(103): -20.9	-0.5
2018	DET	MLB	28	457	72	-5.0	.282	-4.2	C(114): -5.0	-0.3
2019	CHA	MLB	29	476	96	20.7	.359	-0.1	C(106): -10.2	1.0
2020	CHA	MLB	30	210	84	3.5	.313	-0.6	C -4	0.0

James McCann, continued

Batted Ball Distribution

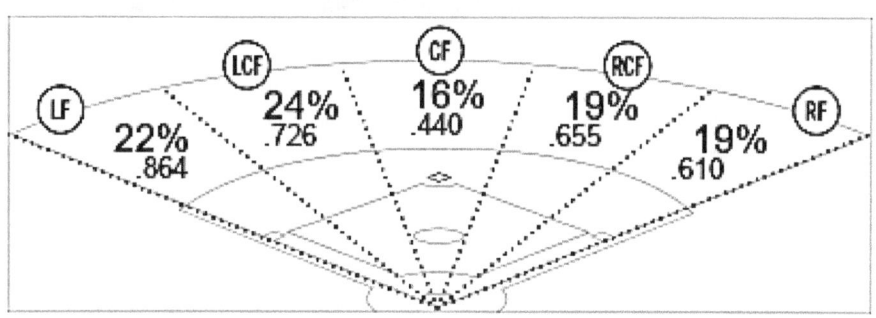

Strike Zone vs LHP   **Strike Zone vs RHP**

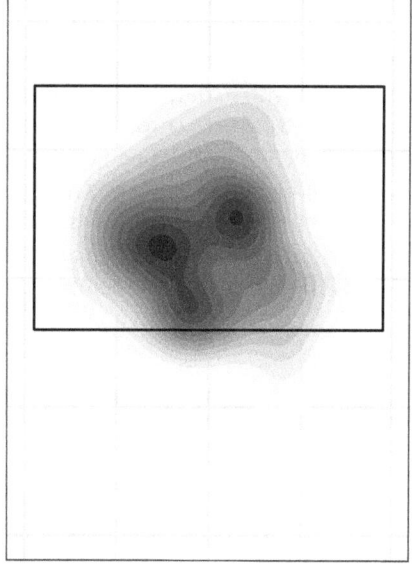

Danny Mendick MI

Born: 09/28/93 Age: 26 Bats: R Throws: R
Height: 5'10" Weight: 189 Origin: Round 22, 2015 Draft (#652 overall)

YEAR	TEAM	LVL	AGE	PA	R	2B	3B	HR	RBI	BB	K	SB	CS	AVG/OBP/SLG
2017	WNS	A+	23	305	45	18	4	7	30	31	40	11	4	.289/.373/.468
2017	BIR	AA	23	165	14	5	0	3	21	17	27	1	2	.197/.280/.293
2018	BIR	AA	24	529	62	25	0	14	59	57	90	20	10	.247/.340/.395
2019	CHR	AAA	25	558	75	26	1	17	64	66	96	19	8	.279/.368/.444
2019	CHA	MLB	25	40	6	0	0	2	4	1	11	0	0	.308/.325/.462
2020	CHA	MLB	26	315	33	14	0	9	34	27	71	4	2	.236/.309/.381

Comparables: Billy Hunter, Kelby Tomlinson, Cliff Pennington

Mendick made his major-league debut before he made his BP Annual debut—and not because of some sort of unforeseeable crisis of White Sox infield depth, either. To trudge through the minors on merit-based promotions and sneak below the radar, Mendick needed to have it all. He's small—generously listed at 5-foot-10—which pushes any notion of even average raw power aside. Unlike the similarly diminutive Madrigal, Mendick doesn't have a standout tool to speak of, getting by on average straight-line speed and making a typical hit tool play up with a mature approach. Additionally, Mendick's big-league plate appearance total only surpassed his advanced age (26) in the final week of the 2019 season, and he has been tasked with proving he was more than just an old guy whipping up on youngsters his entire career. After two years at junior college, Mendick spent two years at Massachusetts-Lowell before he was picked as a 22nd-round senior signing, and then spent another year as an org soldier bouncing between affiliates, emphasizing the primary reason he took this long to get a book comment: no one ever thought he was good enough to make it this far.

YEAR	TEAM	LVL	AGE	PA	DRC+	VORP	BABIP	BRR	FRAA	WARP
2017	WNS	A+	23	305	139	24.8	.315	1.3	2B(45): 5.8, SS(25): -1.6	2.8
2017	BIR	AA	23	165	79	1.0	.222	0.4	SS(34): 5.3, 2B(7): -0.8	0.9
2018	BIR	AA	24	529	110	34.3	.275	1.4	SS(131): -4.2	2.7
2019	CHR	AAA	25	558	102	14.7	.313	0.3	2B(48): 4.2, SS(41): 2.4	2.8
2019	CHA	MLB	25	40	88	1.0	.385	0.0	SS(5): 0.0, 3B(3): 0.7	0.1
2020	CHA	MLB	26	315	84	4.0	.285	-0.4	2B 2, 3B 1	0.8

Danny Mendick, continued

Batted Ball Distribution

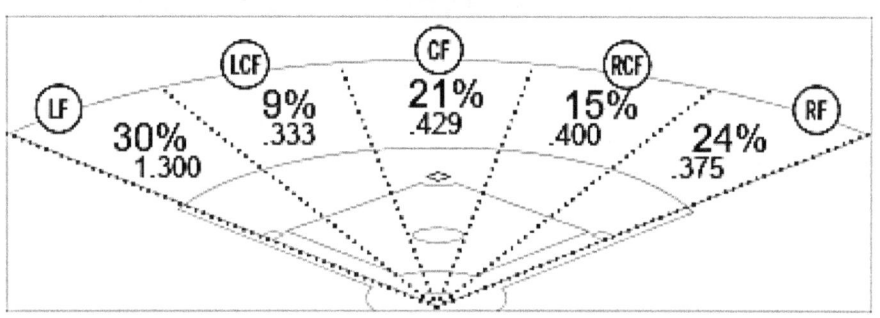

Strike Zone vs LHP

Strike Zone vs RHP

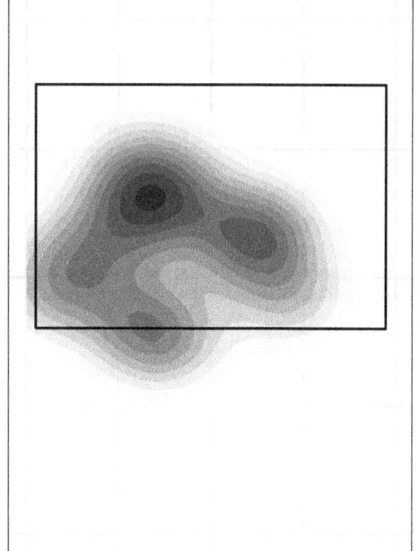

Chicago White Sox 2020

Yoán Moncada 3B
Born: 05/27/95 Age: 25 Bats: B Throws: R
Height: 6'2" Weight: 205 Origin: International Free Agent, 2015

YEAR	TEAM	LVL	AGE	PA	R	2B	3B	HR	RBI	BB	K	SB	CS	AVG/OBP/SLG
2017	CHR	AAA	22	361	57	9	3	12	36	49	102	17	8	.282/.377/.447
2017	CHA	MLB	22	231	31	8	2	8	22	29	74	3	2	.231/.338/.412
2018	CHA	MLB	23	650	73	32	6	17	61	67	217	12	6	.235/.315/.400
2019	CHA	MLB	24	559	83	34	5	25	79	40	154	10	3	.315/.367/.548
2020	CHA	MLB	25	595	76	25	3	27	83	53	170	22	8	.263/.334/.473

Comparables: Gil McDougald, Evan Longoria, Willie Greene

Chances are, the White Sox would have figured out a way to make Manny Machado and Yoán Moncada work in the same infield in some fashion. (What a harrowing challenge that would've been for manager Rick Renteria.) In the meantime, the Sox responded to their failed Machado bid by moving Moncada to Machado's position and watching him outplay the former All-Star. After fetishizing patience to the point of passivity (and a near-record setting number of strikeouts), Moncada turned his in-zone aggression all the way up in 2019. He partly unlocked elite hand speed and plus raw power that was lying fallow as he stared at two-strike fastballs on the outside corner in large quantities, and he was partly rewarded with some of the nuttiest batted-ball luck seen this decade. Think of it as the universe winking at Moncada for embracing the approach that was always best for him—and man, think of how good it would have been to flank him with Machado.

YEAR	TEAM	LVL	AGE	PA	DRC+	VORP	BABIP	BRR	FRAA	WARP
2017	CHR	AAA	22	361	130	16.4	.379	-0.1	2B(80): 1.4	2.2
2017	CHA	MLB	22	231	92	4.5	.325	-0.7	2B(54): 5.8	1.0
2018	CHA	MLB	23	650	89	15.1	.344	-0.4	2B(149): -12.7	-0.2
2019	CHA	MLB	24	559	123	38.5	.406	3.5	3B(129): 10.3	5.1
2020	CHA	MLB	25	595	108	21.3	.336	0.9	3B 4	2.6

Yoán Moncada, continued

Batted Ball Distribution

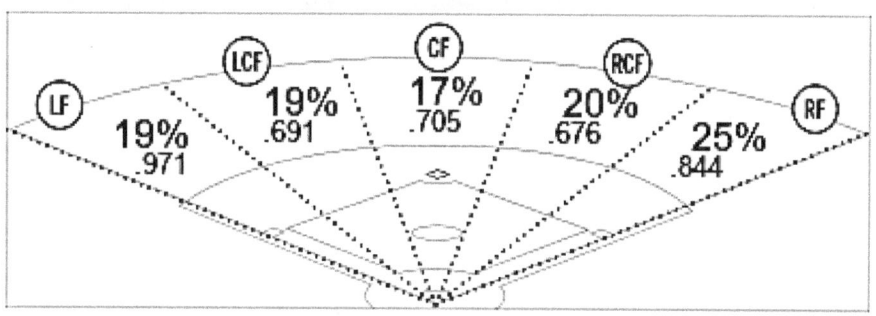

Strike Zone vs LHP   **Strike Zone vs RHP**

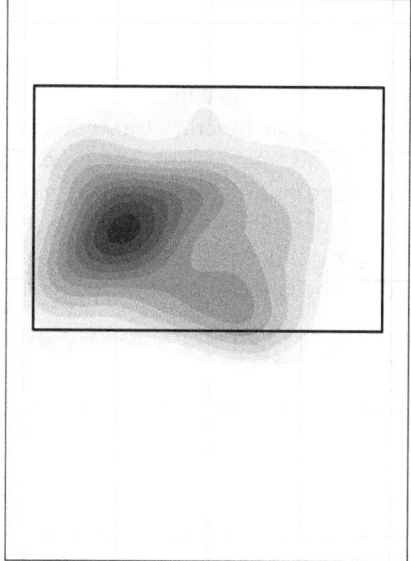

Manny Bañuelos LHP

Born: 03/13/91 Age: 29 Bats: R Throws: L
Height: 5'10" Weight: 215 Origin: International Free Agent, 2008

YEAR	TEAM	LVL	AGE	W	L	SV	G	GS	IP	H	HR	BB/9	K/9	K	GB%	BABIP
2017	SLC	AAA	26	5	6	0	39	9	95	107	4	4.6	8.1	85	48%	.350
2018	OKL	AAA	27	9	7	0	31	18	108^2	109	10	3.5	10.5	127	45%	.349
2019	WNS	A+	28	0	0	0	2	2	8^2	14	1	4.2	10.4	10	48%	.464
2019	CHA	MLB	28	3	4	0	16	8	50^2	60	12	5.9	7.8	44	37%	.331
2020	CHA	MLB	29	2	2	0	33	0	35	37	7	4.1	7.6	29	39%	.296

Comparables: Chris Seddon, John Lamb, Greg Smith

For every Rich Hill—a formerly ballyhooed prospect lefty beset by injuries and setbacks, who really just needed a prolonged break to get healthy, an opportunity and maybe a tweak or two to unlock their dormant talent—there are a legion of stories like Manny Bañuelos. Tommy John surgery, subsequent setbacks and a myriad of other elbow ailments that put many years between the baseball world and the last time they saw him at the height of his powers. Finally afforded the opportunity to rehab by the Angels, and after quietly thriving in Triple-A for a loaded Dodgers organization that didn't need to take a chance on him, the White Sox figured they'd give Bañuelos some run in a rebuilding year. In return they got what they probably should have expected based on his track record. There were some brief glimpses of ability, multiple trips to the injured list for his throwing shoulder, and some true stat-destroying shellackings in moments where he seemed less than 100 percent—all making for a fairly infuriating total package. There's talent in there, though, and with any luck he'll find himself on the Rich side of the hill.

YEAR	TEAM	LVL	AGE	WHIP	ERA	DRA	WARP	MPH	FB%	WHF	CSP
2017	SLC	AAA	26	1.64	4.93	5.13	0.3				
2018	OKL	AAA	27	1.39	3.73	4.35	1.4				
2019	WNS	A+	28	2.08	4.15	6.85	-0.2				
2019	CHA	MLB	28	1.84	6.93	8.41	-1.5	93.9	47.4	10.6	47
2020	CHA	MLB	29	1.52	5.53	5.43	-0.1	93.2	47.4	10.6	47

Manny Bañuelos, continued

Pitch Shape vs LHH

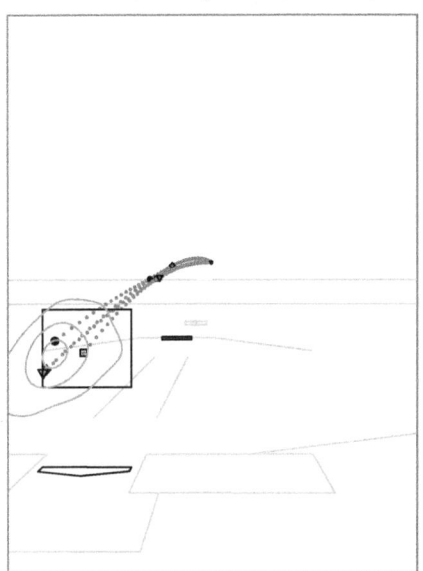

Pitch Shape vs RHH

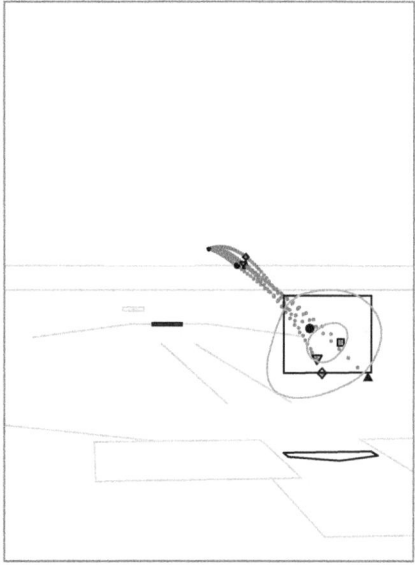

Aaron Bummer LHP

Born: 09/21/93 Age: 26 Bats: L Throws: L
Height: 6'3" Weight: 200 Origin: Round 19, 2014 Draft (#558 overall)

YEAR	TEAM	LVL	AGE	W	L	SV	G	GS	IP	H	HR	BB/9	K/9	K	GB%	BABIP
2017	WNS	A+	23	0	2	2	8	0	11	10	2	2.5	12.3	15	59%	.296
2017	BIR	AA	23	1	3	3	17	1	33	29	2	4.4	9.3	34	56%	.318
2017	CHA	MLB	23	1	3	0	30	0	22	13	4	6.1	7.0	17	57%	.167
2018	CHR	AAA	24	2	3	0	31	0	30^2	27	0	3.2	8.8	30	67%	.310
2018	CHA	MLB	24	0	1	0	37	0	31^2	40	1	2.8	9.9	35	62%	.402
2019	CHR	AAA	25	0	0	0	5	0	7^2	7	0	2.3	7.0	6	96%	.304
2019	CHA	MLB	25	0	0	1	58	0	67^2	43	4	3.2	8.0	60	71%	.228
2020	CHA	MLB	26	3	3	4	59	0	62	56	6	3.6	8.9	61	68%	.293

Comparables: Jerry Blevins, Paul Fry, Eric Stout

Scrolling through an article at his locker about rising batting averages against fastballs during his breakout season, Bummer smirked and quipped that it seemed like great news for him: someone who throws a heater around 80 percent of the time. Prompted by an ugly spring, Bummer mostly ditched his slider for a cutter that he could more consistently locate. He then went through entire innings doing nothing but pounding sinkers. He struck out fewer hitters, walked more, and basically tried to do every outmoded pitching tactic all at once. It worked amazingly well, perhaps because all the cautionary notions about throwing sinkers and striving for weak contact apply to pitchers who are throwing inferior versions of the 95-mph bowling ball Bummer tosses from a lefty slinging motion. Like the best years of Matt Thornton on the South Side a decade before him, if your fastball is good enough—and maybe if you throw it from the left side—then predictability and trends mean about as much as a pot of beans on a Sunday.

YEAR	TEAM	LVL	AGE	WHIP	ERA	DRA	WARP	MPH	FB%	WHF	CSP
2017	WNS	A+	23	1.18	4.91	3.40	0.2				
2017	BIR	AA	23	1.36	3.00	4.87	0.0				
2017	CHA	MLB	23	1.27	4.50	5.95	-0.2	95.1	61	11.1	42.1
2018	CHR	AAA	24	1.24	2.64	3.82	0.5				
2018	CHA	MLB	24	1.58	4.26	3.71	0.4	95.2	65.9	10.5	48.5
2019	CHR	AAA	25	1.17	2.35	3.49	0.2				
2019	CHA	MLB	25	0.99	2.13	2.99	1.7	97.5	76.1	11.4	50.8
2020	CHA	MLB	26	1.30	3.58	3.81	0.9	96.3	72.6	11.3	48.7

Aaron Bummer, continued

Pitch Shape vs LHH

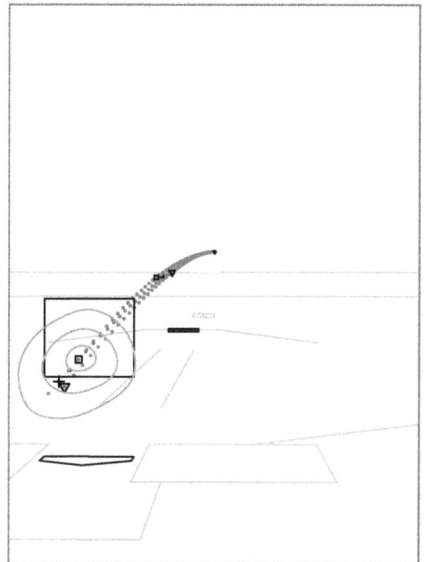

Pitch Shape vs RHH

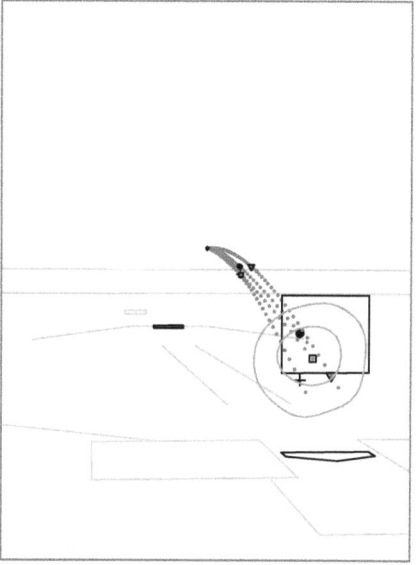

Type	Frequency	Velocity	H Movement	V Movement
● Fastball	5.1%	95.3 [108]	5.6 [106]	-22.3 [83]
☐ Sinker	71.0%	95.9 [117]	10.8 [112]	-23.7 [88]
+ Cutter	14.9%	89 [102]	-2 [101]	-29.3 [80]
▲ Changeup				
✕ Splitter				
▽ Slider	8.6%	85.4 [104]	-7.1 [109]	-34 [97]
◇ Curveball				
✦ Slow Curveball				
✱ Knuckleball				
▼ Screwball				

Dylan Cease RHP

Born: 12/28/95 Age: 24 Bats: R Throws: R
Height: 6'2" Weight: 190 Origin: Round 6, 2014 Draft (#169 overall)

YEAR	TEAM	LVL	AGE	W	L	SV	G	GS	IP	H	HR	BB/9	K/9	K	GB%	BABIP
2017	SBN	A	21	1	2	0	13	13	51²	39	2	4.5	12.9	74	46%	.339
2017	KAN	A	21	0	8	0	9	9	41²	35	1	3.9	11.2	52	43%	.330
2018	WNS	A+	22	9	2	0	13	13	71²	52	5	3.5	10.3	82	50%	.273
2018	BIR	AA	22	3	0	0	10	10	52¹	30	3	3.8	13.4	78	50%	.273
2019	CHR	AAA	23	5	2	0	15	15	68¹	75	4	4.2	9.6	73	55%	.370
2019	CHA	MLB	23	4	7	0	14	14	73	78	15	4.3	10.0	81	46%	.326
2020	CHA	MLB	24	6	5	0	16	16	86	82	13	4.4	9.5	91	47%	.302

Comparables: Hunter Wood, Kyle McGowin, John Gant

It's rare that a pitcher's major-league debut comes in a season where he never seems to get hot for any stretch of time. But such was Cease's 2019, in which his promotion to Chicago was preordained and continued apace despite control and fastball spin issues that never seemed conquered for a period longer than two weeks. He still threw hard, still spun offspeed pitches that fell off the table, and still remained well-regarded. Now that he's a big leaguer, Cease's days of being evaluated for potential—for flashing the look of an upper-90s fastball with three swing-and-miss secondaries—are over; heading forward, it's all about track record. Heretofore, he's proven he can dominate the Tigers, which, since they promoted him from Triple-A, seems like something the White Sox already knew.

YEAR	TEAM	LVL	AGE	WHIP	ERA	DRA	WARP	MPH	FB%	WHF	CSP
2017	SBN	A	21	1.26	2.79	3.65	1.0				
2017	KAN	A	21	1.27	3.89	4.00	0.6				
2018	WNS	A+	22	1.12	2.89	3.34	1.7				
2018	BIR	AA	22	0.99	1.72	2.52	1.7				
2019	CHR	AAA	23	1.57	4.48	4.50	1.5				
2019	CHA	MLB	23	1.55	5.79	5.28	0.4	98.4	51.5	11.6	42.3
2020	CHA	MLB	24	1.44	4.56	4.59	0.9	98.2	53.1	11.9	43.6

Dylan Cease, continued

Pitch Shape vs LHH

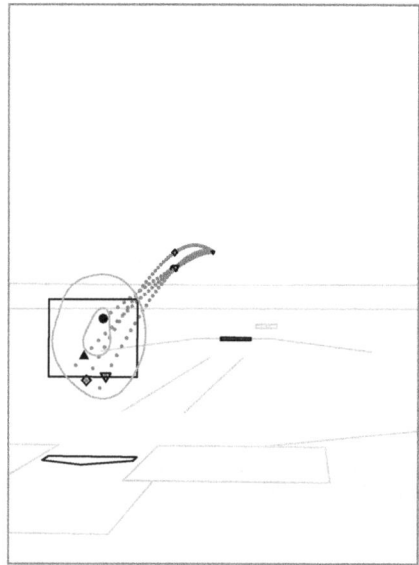

Pitch Shape vs RHH

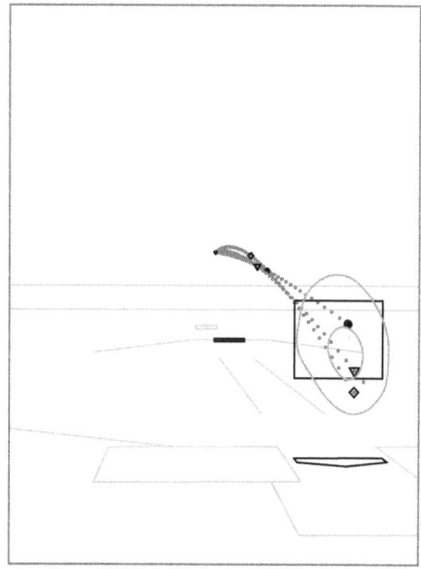

Type	Frequency	Velocity	H Movement	V Movement
● Fastball	51.5%	96.6 [112]	-1.5 [124]	-13.3 [107]
□ Sinker				
+ Cutter				
▲ Changeup	9.0%	83.4 [93]	-1 [147]	-23.2 [112]
✕ Splitter				
▽ Slider	20.9%	84.8 [102]	5.1 [100]	-37.8 [86]
◇ Curveball	18.5%	79.6 [103]	5.9 [94]	-55.2 [84]
⊕ Slow Curveball				
✳ Knuckleball				
▼ Screwball				

Chicago White Sox 2020

Steve Cishek RHP

Born: 06/18/86   Age: 34   Bats: R   Throws: R
Height: 6'6"   Weight: 215   Origin: Round 5, 2007 Draft (#166 overall)

YEAR	TEAM	LVL	AGE	W	L	SV	G	GS	IP	H	HR	BB/9	K/9	K	GB%	BABIP
2017	SEA	MLB	31	1	1	1	23	0	20	13	3	3.2	6.8	15	61%	.185
2017	TBA	MLB	31	2	1	0	26	0	24²	13	0	2.6	9.5	26	52%	.220
2018	CHN	MLB	32	4	3	4	80	0	70¹	45	5	3.6	10.0	78	49%	.238
2019	CHN	MLB	33	4	6	7	70	0	64	48	7	4.1	8.0	57	50%	.246
2020	CHA	MLB	34	2	2	0	48	0	51	44	8	3.5	8.8	50	48%	.268

Comparables: Brad Brach, Rafael Soriano, Brian Wilson

In the era of power-armed strikeout pitchers, Cishek has found a home in the bigs as a rubber-armed, quirky, change-of-pace pitcher. One problem: His command is becoming an issue, as his walk rate has gone from 8.1 percent to 9.7 percent, to 10.9 percent over the last three years. He still gets loads of groundballs, but he'll need to stop putting runners on base as he ages and (presumably) misses fewer bats. Can he reverse the trend?

YEAR	TEAM	LVL	AGE	WHIP	ERA	DRA	WARP	MPH	FB%	WHF	CSP
2017	SEA	MLB	31	1.00	3.15	4.78	0.1	92.3	51.5	8.2	46.5
2017	TBA	MLB	31	0.81	1.09	3.41	0.5	92.8	49.5	13.7	44.3
2018	CHN	MLB	32	1.04	2.18	4.68	0.2	92.7	61.6	12	46.7
2019	CHN	MLB	33	1.20	2.95	4.08	0.9	92.7	59.2	9.8	44.3
2020	CHA	MLB	34	1.26	3.87	4.16	0.7	91.6	57.7	10.7	44.7

Steve Cishek, continued

Pitch Shape vs LHH

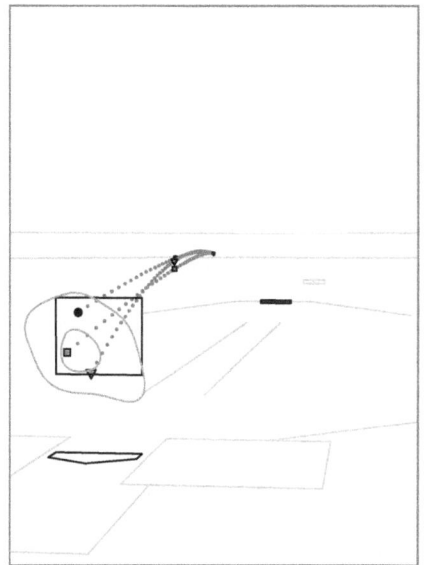

Pitch Shape vs RHH

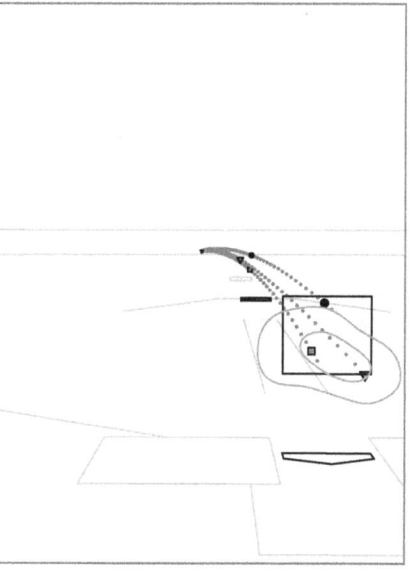

Type	Frequency	Velocity	H Movement	V Movement
● Fastball	13.7%	91 [96]	-10 [86]	-21.9 [84]
☐ Sinker	45.4%	91 [92]	-14.7 [87]	-26.6 [78]
+ Cutter				
▲ Changeup				
✕ Splitter				
▽ Slider	40.0%	79.2 [78]	10.2 [122]	-40.2 [80]
◇ Curveball				
⊕ Slow Curveball				
✳ Knuckleball				
▼ Screwball				

Chicago White Sox 2020

Alex Colomé   RHP
Born: 12/31/88   Age: 31   Bats: R   Throws: R
Height: 6'1"   Weight: 220   Origin: International Free Agent, 2007

YEAR	TEAM	LVL	AGE	W	L	SV	G	GS	IP	H	HR	BB/9	K/9	K	GB%	BABIP
2017	TBA	MLB	28	2	3	47	65	0	66²	57	4	3.1	7.8	58	50%	.275
2018	TBA	MLB	29	2	5	11	23	0	21²	24	1	3.3	9.6	23	55%	.354
2018	SEA	MLB	29	5	0	1	47	0	46¹	35	6	2.5	9.5	49	42%	.254
2019	CHA	MLB	30	4	5	30	62	0	61	42	7	3.4	8.1	55	45%	.215
2020	CHA	MLB	31	3	3	36	59	0	62	54	9	3.1	8.8	61	45%	.273

Comparables: Cody Martin, Adam Warren, Aaron Blair

In the three seasons since his deserved 2016 trip to the All-Star Game, Colomé's strikeout rates have yo-yo'd, his sweeping and diving cutter has and hasn't racked up harmless ground balls for various stretches, and he's bounced in and out of a closer role that's highly coveted for someone whose salary is at least partially mapped out by arbitration projections.)DRA, to its credit, has seen the same guy three years running.) There's decent, but not exceptional control, he's not a wormkiller, but more likely to get someone to roll-over than most. Colomé doesn't get hammered, but is no wizard of weak contact. He's a bit better than your typical reliever, which means when he's rolling, he can get high-leverage outs. It also means that the ideal bullpen would task him with getting only medium-leverage ones, putting him in a position to overperform rather than disappoint. The White Sox bullpen is not that ideal bullpen.

YEAR	TEAM	LVL	AGE	WHIP	ERA	DRA	WARP	MPH	FB%	WHF	CSP
2017	TBA	MLB	28	1.20	3.24	3.97	0.9	96.2	32.7	12.4	46.8
2018	TBA	MLB	29	1.48	4.15	3.91	0.3	96.3	36.8	16	48.9
2018	SEA	MLB	29	1.04	2.53	3.97	0.5	96.8	36.8	15	45.5
2019	CHA	MLB	30	1.07	2.80	3.99	0.9	95.7	29	14.5	45.6
2020	CHA	MLB	31	1.22	3.56	3.80	0.9	95.3	32.5	14.2	46

Alex Colomé, continued

Pitch Shape vs LHH

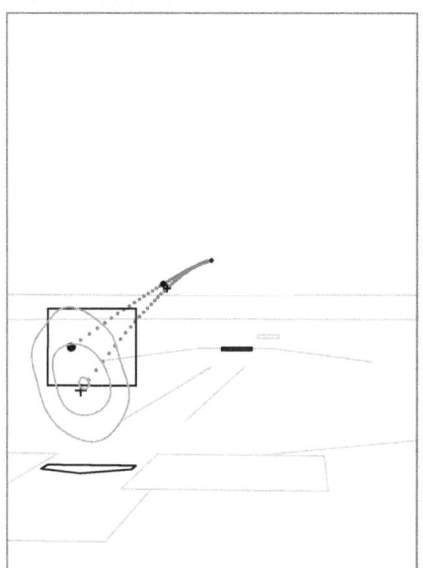

Pitch Shape vs RHH

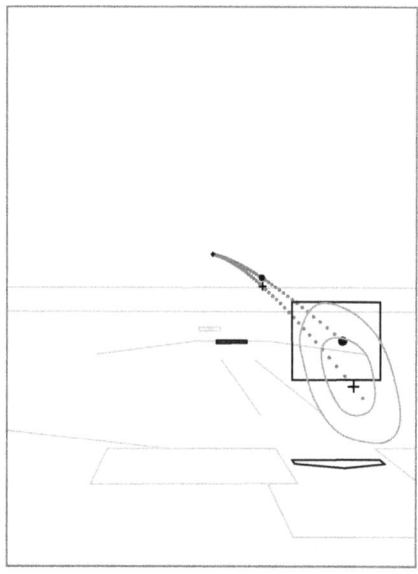

Type	Frequency	Velocity	H Movement	V Movement
● Fastball	29.0%	94.7 [107]	-2.9 [118]	-11.5 [112]
☐ Sinker				
+ Cutter	71.0%	90.7 [113]	1.2 [96]	-22.9 [104]
▲ Changeup				
✕ Splitter				
▽ Slider				
◇ Curveball				
⊕ Slow Curveball				
✱ Knuckleball				
▼ Screwball				

Jimmy Cordero RHP

Born: 10/19/91 Age: 28 Bats: R Throws: R
Height: 6'4" Weight: 222 Origin: International Free Agent, 2012

YEAR	TEAM	LVL	AGE	W	L	SV	G	GS	IP	H	HR	BB/9	K/9	K	GB%	BABIP
2017	HAR	AA	25	2	6	0	41	0	51^1	52	7	6.7	7.0	40	53%	.290
2018	SYR	AAA	26	4	1	6	41	0	46	43	0	4.3	10.4	53	55%	.333
2018	WAS	MLB	26	1	2	0	22	0	19	23	2	5.7	5.7	12	57%	.318
2019	CHR	AAA	27	3	1	4	13	0	17^2	14	0	1.0	7.1	14	72%	.275
2019	FRE	AAA	27	0	1	3	12	0	15	17	3	5.4	10.2	17	53%	.333
2019	CHA	MLB	27	1	0	0	30	0	36	24	3	2.8	7.8	31	62%	.226
2019	TOR	MLB	27	0	1	0	1	0	1^1	2	1	0.0	0.0	0	40%	.250
2020	CHA	MLB	28	1	1	0	27	0	28	26	3	3.8	9.0	28	58%	.292

Comparables: Kyle Martin, Branden Pinder, Tayler Scott

Cordero has huge biceps, a pathological hatred of sleeves (he rolls them up when he pitches), and (very) easily touches 98 mph with a sinker that generates heaps of ground balls. That he's changed teams six times in his young career (three times in 2019 alone) seems like a flagrant display of ignorance of how cool it is to watch a pitcher huck high-90s heaters with his guns out. But given how often Cordero was re-gifted (and whom he was re-gifted by), you would have expected a more arduous reclamation project than he proved to be. He was…fine. He torched Triple-A like legit big leaguers tend to do, and threw enough strikes at high enough speeds to balance out how non-particular he was about where in the zone he located them. If he continues to do that, he should remain in the majors, tease some possibility of more, and never have to wear his sleeves down again.

YEAR	TEAM	LVL	AGE	WHIP	ERA	DRA	WARP	MPH	FB%	WHF	CSP
2017	HAR	AA	25	1.75	6.84	6.89	-1.3				
2018	SYR	AAA	26	1.41	1.96	4.55	0.3				
2018	WAS	MLB	26	1.84	5.68	6.42	-0.3	100.4	61.8	12.3	43.8
2019	CHR	AAA	27	0.91	0.51	2.16	0.7				
2019	FRE	AAA	27	1.73	6.00	4.27	0.3				
2019	CHA	MLB	27	0.97	2.75	3.47	0.7	99.8	68.6	15.4	49.8
2019	TOR	MLB	27	1.50	6.75	6.21	0.0	98.2	53.3	6.7	57.9
2020	CHA	MLB	28	1.32	3.84	3.99	0.4	99.3	66.5	14.3	47.5

Jimmy Cordero, continued

Pitch Shape vs LHH

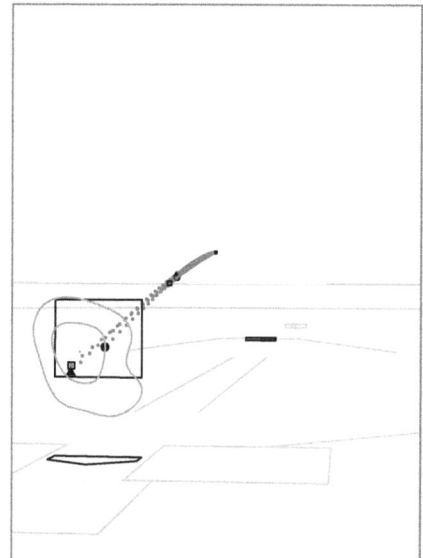

Pitch Shape vs RHH

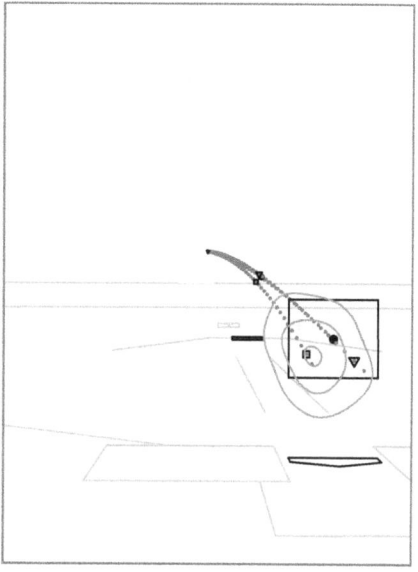

Type	Frequency	Velocity	H Movement	V Movement
● Fastball	19.0%	97.8 [115]	-4.3 [111]	-14.4 [104]
☐ Sinker	49.2%	97.6 [126]	-12.8 [99]	-17 [112]
+ Cutter				
▲ Changeup	17.6%	88.7 [112]	-10.4 [104]	-24.1 [110]
✕ Splitter				
▽ Slider	7.0%	91.1 [128]	1.2 [84]	-24.3 [125]
◇ Curveball	7.2%	83.7 [117]	2.3 [79]	-40.3 [115]
⊕ Slow Curveball				
✳ Knuckleball				
▼ Screwball				

Chicago White Sox 2020

Odrisamer Despaigne   RHP
Born: 04/04/87   Age: 33   Bats: R   Throws: R
Height: 6'0"   Weight: 200   Origin: International Free Agent, 2014

YEAR	TEAM	LVL	AGE	W	L	SV	G	GS	IP	H	HR	BB/9	K/9	K	GB%	BABIP
2017	NWO	AAA	30	2	4	2	20	10	70	62	6	3.1	6.3	49	52%	.271
2017	MIA	MLB	30	2	3	1	18	8	58^1	57	3	3.7	4.8	31	38%	.280
2018	NWO	AAA	31	2	3	2	13	4	43^1	52	0	2.5	8.3	40	44%	.380
2018	LAA	MLB	31	0	3	0	8	4	18^2	30	3	5.3	8.2	17	44%	.415
2018	MIA	MLB	31	2	0	0	11	1	20^1	22	1	3.5	8.0	18	41%	.333
2019	CHR	AAA	32	5	4	0	16	14	83	83	6	3.0	9.1	84	50%	.333
2019	LOU	AAA	32	3	2	0	8	8	41^1	40	5	3.5	8.7	40	53%	.310
2019	CHA	MLB	32	0	2	0	3	3	13^1	24	3	4.7	4.7	7	28%	.420
2020	CHA	MLB	33	2	2	0	33	0	35	40	6	3.7	5.8	23	43%	.300

Comparables: Alex Wilson, Eric O'Flaherty, Chris Rusin

If you need someone to be an innings-eating lynchpin of a Triple-A rotation, serving as both a key figure in an International League playoff drive and providing a small thrill to fans as guy who does a vaguely convincing El Duque impersonation, Odrisamer is your man. If you want someone to perplex your major-league roster and coaching staff with an oddly lax pregame warmup routine that seems to make everyone ask "My God, does he know what time it is?" before unleashing an astonishingly wide arsenal of poorly commanded and eminently hittable pitches, Odrisamer, regrettably, is also your man. Teams never seem to truly need the former, and so quickly grow weary of the latter, that Despaigne's professional future figures to be at least as transient as his already fairly wacky 2019.

YEAR	TEAM	LVL	AGE	WHIP	ERA	DRA	WARP	MPH	FB%	WHF	CSP
2017	NWO	AAA	30	1.23	3.09	3.39	1.7				
2017	MIA	MLB	30	1.39	4.01	5.17	0.2	94.4	84.3	8	47.5
2018	NWO	AAA	31	1.48	4.36	4.74	0.3				
2018	LAA	MLB	31	2.20	8.20	6.74	-0.4	95.3	67.4	9.7	48.9
2018	MIA	MLB	31	1.48	5.31	4.61	0.1	94.6	67.4	14.6	43.2
2019	CHR	AAA	32	1.34	3.25	4.42	1.8				
2019	LOU	AAA	32	1.35	3.92	5.14	0.6				
2019	CHA	MLB	32	2.33	9.45	10.03	-0.6	94.9	74.8	5.9	45.9
2020	CHA	MLB	33	1.55	5.73	5.58	-0.1	93.7	74.6	9.2	45.9

Odrisamer Despaigne, continued

Pitch Shape vs LHH

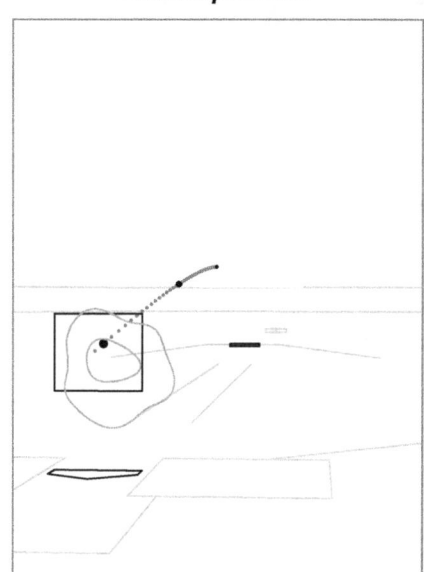

Pitch Shape vs RHH

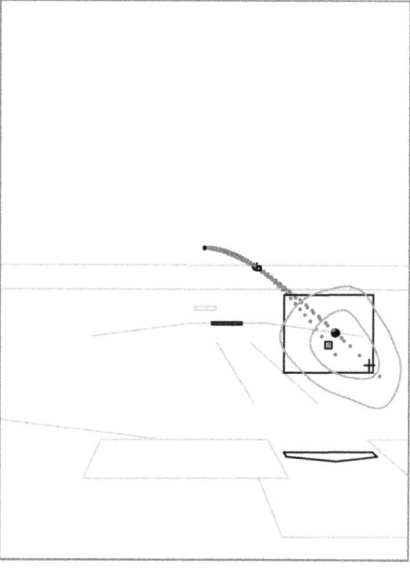

Chicago White Sox 2020

Jace Fry LHP
Born: 07/09/93   Age: 26   Bats: L   Throws: L
Height: 6'1"   Weight: 190   Origin: Round 3, 2014 Draft (#77 overall)

YEAR	TEAM	LVL	AGE	W	L	SV	G	GS	IP	H	HR	BB/9	K/9	K	GB%	BABIP
2017	BIR	AA	23	2	1	3	33	0	45^1	36	1	4.8	10.3	52	59%	.307
2017	CHA	MLB	23	0	0	0	11	0	6^2	12	1	6.8	4.1	3	39%	.407
2018	CHR	AAA	24	0	0	0	5	0	6^2	3	1	0.0	14.9	11	54%	.167
2018	CHA	MLB	24	2	3	4	59	1	51^1	37	4	3.5	12.3	70	47%	.277
2019	CHA	MLB	25	3	4	0	68	0	55	44	7	7.0	11.1	68	58%	.292
2020	CHA	MLB	26	3	3	0	53	0	57	46	7	4.6	10.8	68	52%	.285

Comparables: Rex Brothers, Tony Sipp, Antonio Bastardo

It's seldom fair to compare a pitcher like Fry—a mercurial second-year lefty reliever in a rebuilding team's bullpen—to a future Hall of Famer like Zack Greinke, but humor us for a moment. That Fry threw about a quarter as many innings as Greinke did in 2019, yet issued a good deal more walks than Greinke (along with 12 other qualified starters) is a good encapsulation of his sophomore struggles. Fry's best pitch is a cutter, and part of his appeal is having a five-pitch mix of which no offering moves in a straight line. Seeing as how no pitcher with more than 50 frames walked a higher rate, that liveliness may double as his downfall.

YEAR	TEAM	LVL	AGE	WHIP	ERA	DRA	WARP	MPH	FB%	WHF	CSP
2017	BIR	AA	23	1.32	2.78	4.14	0.4				
2017	CHA	MLB	23	2.55	10.80	5.83	0.0	95.8	68.2	10.8	41.1
2018	CHR	AAA	24	0.45	1.35	1.69	0.3				
2018	CHA	MLB	24	1.11	4.38	2.96	1.2	95.4	34.2	15.3	43.7
2019	CHA	MLB	25	1.58	4.75	4.06	0.8	95.0	25.1	14.7	40.4
2020	CHA	MLB	26	1.32	3.64	3.83	0.8	94.8	31	15.1	42.4

Jace Fry, continued

Pitch Shape vs LHH

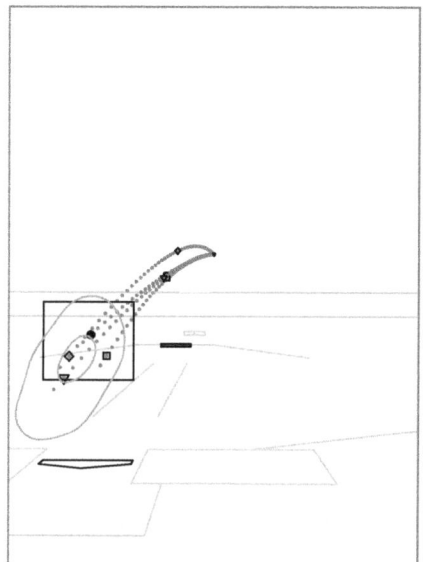

Pitch Shape vs RHH

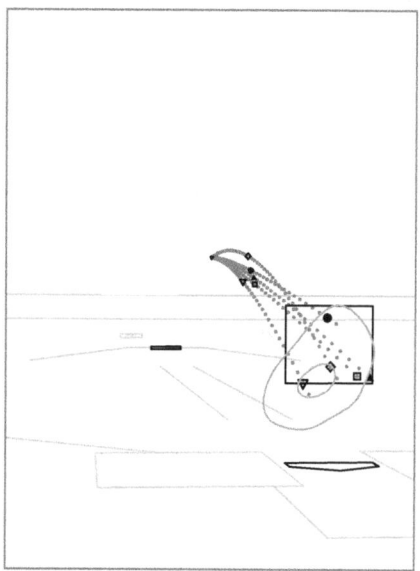

Type	Frequency	Velocity	H Movement	V Movement
● Fastball	12.2%	93 [102]	5.7 [105]	-14.5 [104]
☐ Sinker	12.9%	92.5 [100]	12.5 [101]	-21.5 [96]
+ Cutter				
▲ Changeup	7.0%	86.3 [104]	11.6 [98]	-26.1 [104]
✕ Splitter				
▽ Slider	49.3%	88.5 [117]	-0.3 [80]	-29.2 [111]
◇ Curveball	18.6%	78.6 [100]	-5 [90]	-51.3 [92]
⊕ Slow Curveball				
✳ Knuckleball				
▼ Screwball				

Chicago White Sox 2020

Carson Fulmer RHP
Born: 12/13/93 Age: 26 Bats: R Throws: R
Height: 6'0" Weight: 195 Origin: Round 1, 2015 Draft (#8 overall)

YEAR	TEAM	LVL	AGE	W	L	SV	G	GS	IP	H	HR	BB/9	K/9	K	GB%	BABIP
2017	CHR	AAA	23	7	9	0	25	25	126	132	18	4.6	6.9	96	46%	.297
2017	CHA	MLB	23	3	1	0	7	5	23^1	16	4	5.0	7.3	19	31%	.190
2018	CHR	AAA	24	5	6	0	25	9	67^2	70	10	5.5	8.2	62	40%	.316
2018	CHA	MLB	24	2	4	0	9	8	32^1	37	8	6.7	8.1	29	34%	.296
2019	CHR	AAA	25	1	2	1	24	0	34	31	2	5.6	13.5	51	32%	.372
2019	CHA	MLB	25	1	2	0	20	2	27^1	26	5	6.6	8.2	25	47%	.262
2020	CHA	MLB	26	4	4	0	29	8	64	64	11	5.3	7.8	56	39%	.288

Comparables: Miguel Almonte, Lucas Sims, Chase De Jong

Two of the sharpest innings Fulmer threw in 2019, and maybe even his entire career, came in the 12th and 13th innings of an August victory in Philadelphia that was mostly marked by the unyielding chaos of the five-and-a-half hour affair. Rather than build off of it, he would not pitch in the majors for another month, as he pulled his hamstring trying to run out a would-be infield single while batting for himself in the 14th. This isn't the most telling moment of Fulmer's inability to gain traction since being drafted eighth overall in 2015, just the most recent. He's changed roles, moving to the bullpen; he's changed residencies, moving to Washington so he can train at Driveline's facility during the offseason; but he hasn't yet changed teams. He will. Likely soon.

YEAR	TEAM	LVL	AGE	WHIP	ERA	DRA	WARP	MPH	FB%	WHF	CSP
2017	CHR	AAA	23	1.56	5.79	6.04	-0.5				
2017	CHA	MLB	23	1.24	3.86	7.31	-0.5	94.9	51.8	9.6	46.1
2018	CHR	AAA	24	1.64	5.32	6.24	-0.6				
2018	CHA	MLB	24	1.89	8.07	8.06	-1.0	94.8	55.3	7.3	44.8
2019	CHR	AAA	25	1.53	4.76	3.42	0.9				
2019	CHA	MLB	25	1.68	6.26	6.60	-0.4	95.2	43.9	11.7	45.7
2020	CHA	MLB	26	1.59	5.51	5.31	0.1	94.6	50.8	9.7	46.3

Carson Fulmer, continued

Pitch Shape vs LHH

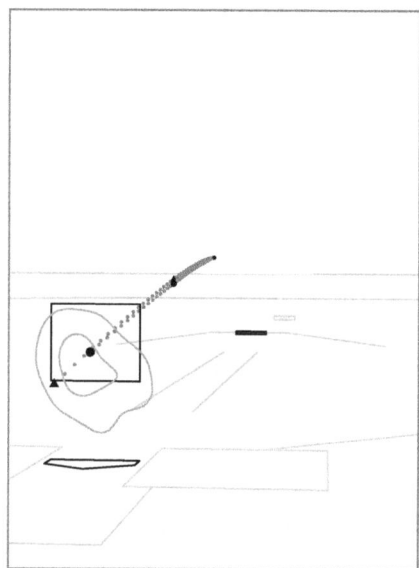

Pitch Shape vs RHH

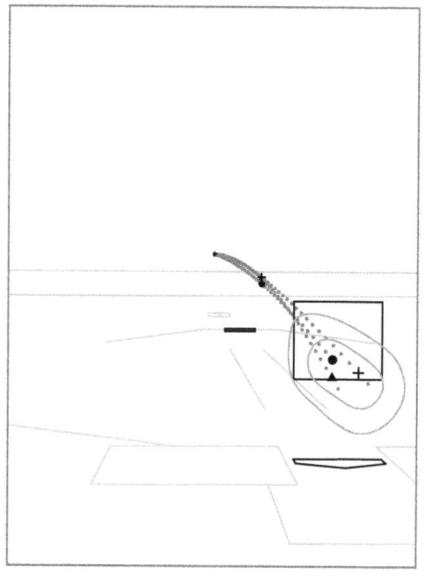

Type	Frequency	Velocity	H Movement	V Movement
● Fastball	43.9%	94 [105]	-5.9 [104]	-12.8 [108]
□ Sinker				
+ Cutter	32.8%	88.4 [98]	4.5 [116]	-27.2 [88]
▲ Changeup	15.7%	86.9 [106]	-12.3 [95]	-26 [104]
✕ Splitter				
▽ Slider				
◇ Curveball	7.7%	83.2 [115]	6.9 [98]	-41.7 [112]
⊕ Slow Curveball				
✳ Knuckleball				
▼ Screwball				

Chicago White Sox 2020

Lucas Giolito   RHP

Born: 07/14/94 Age: 25 Bats: R Throws: R
Height: 6'6" Weight: 245 Origin: Round 1, 2012 Draft (#16 overall)

YEAR	TEAM	LVL	AGE	W	L	SV	G	GS	IP	H	HR	BB/9	K/9	K	GB%	BABIP
2017	CHR	AAA	22	6	10	0	24	24	128^2	122	17	4.1	9.4	134	45%	.312
2017	CHA	MLB	22	3	3	0	7	7	45^1	31	8	2.4	6.8	34	47%	.189
2018	CHA	MLB	23	10	13	0	32	32	173^1	166	27	4.7	6.5	125	45%	.268
2019	CHA	MLB	24	14	9	0	29	29	176^2	131	24	2.9	11.6	228	36%	.273
2020	CHA	MLB	25	12	8	0	28	28	165	141	26	3.6	11.1	204	39%	.290

Comparables: Archie Bradley, José Berríos, Jake Thompson

If you're a 0.9er who listened to his dad get interviewed, or just the type of casual fan who watches enough baseball to hear mention of the top-10 prospects in baseball on a year-to-year basis, Lucas Giolito's ascent to greatness has felt like an inevitability. When it's all said and done, Giolito's 2018 season, where he briefly fashioned himself a sinkerballer as he toggled through different mechanics in a desperate search for a fix, will eventually read as an aberrant blip entirely. That would be a shame because Giolito's dedicated efforts to overhaul his delivery and his mindset—and emerge from inconsistency and uncertainty as a relentless barrage of high-riding four-seamers and unshakable confidence—is the sort of straightforward tale of determined self-improvement that draws us to sports. They provide an easy story that anything is possible if we dedicate ourselves to making it happen. The hard part is actually doing it.

YEAR	TEAM	LVL	AGE	WHIP	ERA	DRA	WARP	MPH	FB%	WHF	CSP
2017	CHR	AAA	22	1.41	4.48	4.89	1.1				
2017	CHA	MLB	22	0.95	2.38	4.27	0.7	94.3	59.8	11.1	46.2
2018	CHA	MLB	23	1.48	6.13	6.58	-2.5	95.0	59.5	9.2	46.8
2019	CHA	MLB	24	1.06	3.41	2.81	5.7	96.7	55	16.1	50.3
2020	CHA	MLB	25	1.25	3.76	3.93	3.0	95.5	58.6	13.1	49.3

Lucas Giolito, continued

Pitch Shape vs LHH
Pitch Shape vs RHH

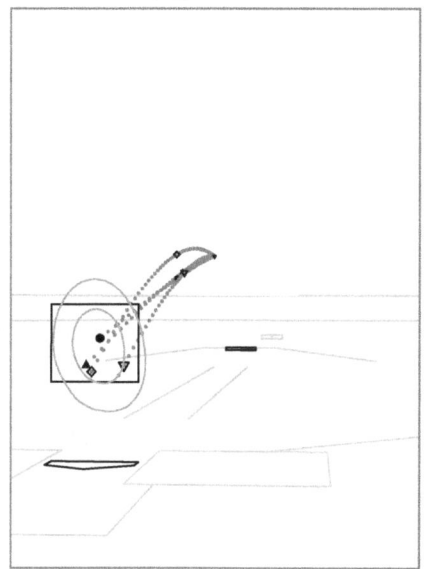
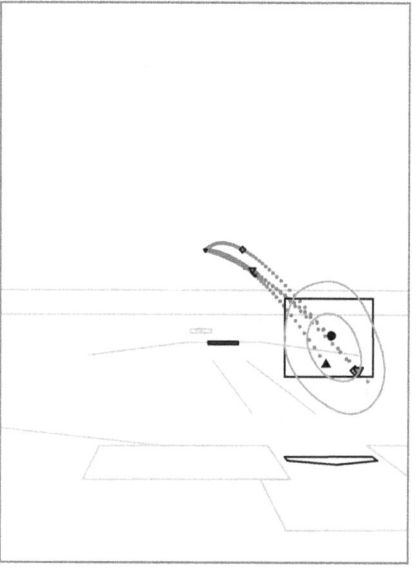

Type	Frequency	Velocity	H Movement	V Movement
● Fastball	55.0%	94.6 [106]	-6.5 [102]	-11 [113]
☐ Sinker				
+ Cutter				
▲ Changeup	26.0%	82 [88]	-8.8 [111]	-25.2 [107]
✕ Splitter				
▽ Slider	14.8%	84.9 [102]	2.7 [91]	-28.5 [113]
◇ Curveball	4.1%	79.9 [104]	6.5 [96]	-52.3 [90]
✦ Slow Curveball				
✲ Knuckleball				
▼ Screwball				

Chicago White Sox 2020

Gio Gonzalez LHP

Born: 09/19/85 Age: 34 Bats: R Throws: L
Height: 6'0" Weight: 205 Origin: Round 1, 2004 Draft (#38 overall)

YEAR	TEAM	LVL	AGE	W	L	SV	G	GS	IP	H	HR	BB/9	K/9	K	GB%	BABIP
2017	WAS	MLB	31	15	9	0	32	32	201	158	21	3.5	8.4	188	48%	.258
2018	WAS	MLB	32	7	11	0	27	27	145^2	153	15	4.3	7.8	126	47%	.319
2018	MIL	MLB	32	3	0	0	5	5	25^1	14	2	3.6	7.8	22	46%	.182
2019	SWB	AAA	33	2	1	0	3	3	15	19	1	3.6	11.4	19	48%	.439
2019	MIL	MLB	33	3	2	0	19	17	87^1	76	9	3.8	8.0	78	47%	.277
2020	CHA	MLB	34	8	6	0	23	23	116	105	18	3.9	7.8	101	47%	.271

Comparables: Jon Lester, Francisco Liriano, David Price

Gonzalez is a good example of how the Brewers profit off the league-wide aversion to 30-something-year-olds. Yes, last year was his age-33 season; yes, his peripherals were decidedly mediocre; and yes, he has middling control at best and a waning fastball. But can you imagine a pitcher like Gonzalez—a longtime, left-handed veteran with his year-to-year consistency—receiving a piddling $2 million in free agency just a decade ago? There's risk management and then there's playing yourself. Gonzalez had some injury problems, but he delivered more value for the Brewers than what they deposited into his bank account. The White Sox took note, signing him to a one-year, $4.5 million contract with an option for 2021.

YEAR	TEAM	LVL	AGE	WHIP	ERA	DRA	WARP	MPH	FB%	WHF	CSP
2017	WAS	MLB	31	1.18	2.96	3.60	4.4	91.8	56.8	9.4	42.3
2018	WAS	MLB	32	1.53	4.57	4.33	1.7	92.0	56.4	9.8	45.8
2018	MIL	MLB	32	0.95	2.13	3.27	0.6	92.2	58.2	12.6	41.2
2019	SWB	AAA	33	1.67	6.00	5.44	0.2				
2019	MIL	MLB	33	1.29	3.50	4.41	1.3	91.1	51.9	11.2	37.1
2020	CHA	MLB	34	1.34	4.10	4.26	1.7	90.6	54.7	10	40.5

Gio Gonzalez, continued

Pitch Shape vs LHH

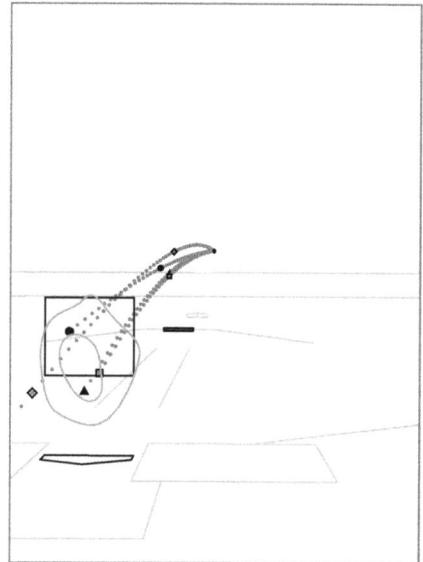

Pitch Shape vs RHH

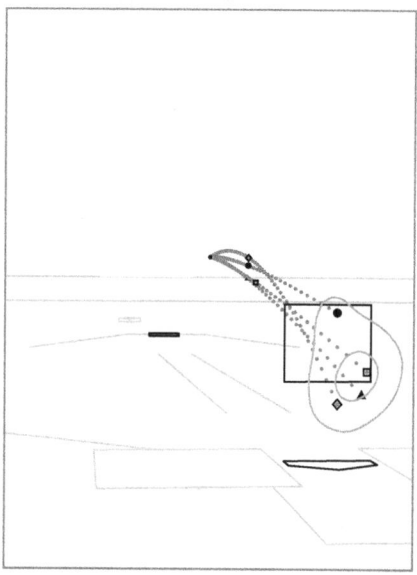

Type	Frequency	Velocity	H Movement	V Movement
● Fastball	27.6%	89.8 [93]	8.4 [93]	-15.6 [101]
☐ Sinker	24.3%	89.2 [82]	13.6 [94]	-20.8 [99]
+ Cutter				
▲ Changeup	31.7%	82.6 [90]	11.8 [97]	-29.5 [94]
✕ Splitter				
▽ Slider				
◇ Curveball	16.4%	75.5 [90]	-9.6 [109]	-58.2 [78]
⊕ Slow Curveball				
✳ Knuckleball				
▼ Screwball				

Tayron Guerrero RHP

Born: 01/09/91 Age: 29 Bats: R Throws: R
Height: 6'8" Weight: 210 Origin: International Free Agent, 2009

YEAR	TEAM	LVL	AGE	W	L	SV	G	GS	IP	H	HR	BB/9	K/9	K	GB%	BABIP
2017	JAX	AA	26	0	1	0	17	0	16	14	3	7.9	12.4	22	41%	.306
2017	NWO	AAA	26	3	2	0	13	0	15¹	12	2	7.0	6.5	11	44%	.217
2018	MIA	MLB	27	1	3	0	60	0	58	64	8	4.7	10.6	68	45%	.354
2019	MIA	MLB	28	1	2	0	52	0	46	42	7	7.0	8.4	43	44%	.282
2020	CHA	MLB	29	1	1	0	11	0	11	12	2	5.7	10.1	13	44%	.325

Comparables: Gregory Infante, Ryne Harper, Hunter Cervenka

There are relievers with dubious command, and then there is Guerrero. That he managed a painful-to-watch walk rate and a pedestrian strikeout rate, all while hurling his 99-mph fastball somewhere in the vicinity of home plate, is a modern marvel. Among relievers who threw at least 40 innings in 2019, Guerrero had the third-highest walk rate and second-worst K/BB percentage. Seemingly the only thing that kept Guerrero on the mound—besides Miami's dearth of solid relievers—was the non-alarming rate at which he surrendered homers, limiting the significance of the walks to merely "very damaging." The 6-foot-8 righty will continue to get more opportunities to harness that fastball for as long as it maintains its radar gun readings, but the Marlins do have more capable arms in the pipeline. Guerrero's time in one of the NL's worst bullpens was short-lived, but he'll always have those highlights for the Wide, Wide, Wide World of Sports.

YEAR	TEAM	LVL	AGE	WHIP	ERA	DRA	WARP	MPH	FB%	WHF	CSP
2017	JAX	AA	26	1.75	3.38	4.80	0.0				
2017	NWO	AAA	26	1.57	5.87	5.41	0.0				
2018	MIA	MLB	27	1.62	5.43	4.80	0.1	102.0	79.2	12.4	49.4
2019	MIA	MLB	28	1.70	6.26	6.04	-0.3	101.8	79.2	14.1	44.8
2020	CHA	MLB	29	1.67	5.72	5.41	0.0	101.2	79.2	13.3	46.9

Tayron Guerrero, continued

Pitch Shape vs LHH

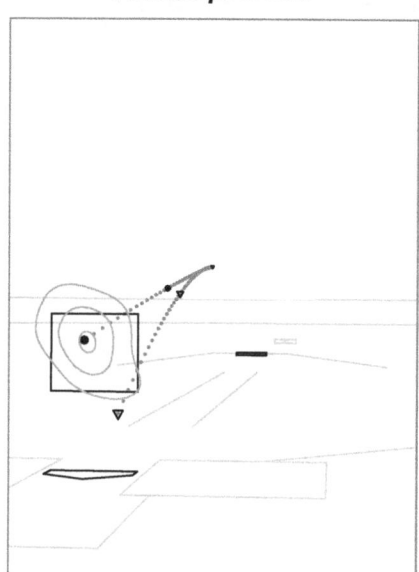

Pitch Shape vs RHH

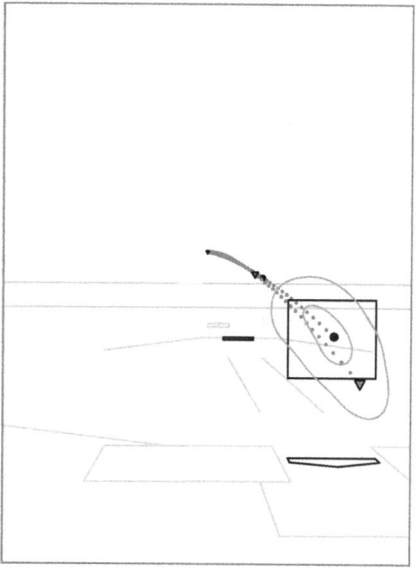

Type	Frequency	Velocity	H Movement	V Movement
● Fastball	79.2%	99.4 [120]	-8.1 [94]	-11.3 [112]
☐ Sinker				
+ Cutter				
▲ Changeup				
✕ Splitter				
▽ Slider	20.4%	87.7 [114]	3.9 [96]	-31.2 [105]
◇ Curveball				
⊕ Slow Curveball				
✱ Knuckleball				
▼ Screwball				

White Sox Player Analysis - 69

Kelvin Herrera RHP

Born: 12/31/89 Age: 30 Bats: R Throws: R
Height: 5'10" Weight: 200 Origin: International Free Agent, 2006

YEAR	TEAM	LVL	AGE	W	L	SV	G	GS	IP	H	HR	BB/9	K/9	K	GB%	BABIP
2017	KCA	MLB	27	3	3	26	64	0	59^1	60	9	3.0	8.5	56	47%	.295
2018	KCA	MLB	28	1	1	14	27	0	25^2	19	2	0.7	7.7	22	39%	.246
2018	WAS	MLB	28	1	2	3	21	0	18^2	24	4	3.9	7.7	16	36%	.333
2019	CHA	MLB	29	3	3	1	57	0	51^1	60	8	4.0	9.3	53	39%	.347
2020	CHA	MLB	30	2	2	0	32	0	34	31	5	3.1	9.2	35	38%	.288

Comparables: Huston Street, Drew Storen, Bruce Sutter

Our 20s are such a fleeting, treasured time. So, then, it was a powerful gesture that Herrera dedicated his 29th year to acting out a telling lesson about the interconnected nature of the human body. After tearing the Lisfranc ligament in his left foot—the plant foot!—to end his 2018 season, Herrera was not able to build up strength in his left leg during his winter, resulting in reduced velocity during the spring. He was making due until all of his careful compensation for his leg led to him tweaking his back (in his 20s!) and spending almost the rest of the season accumulating the worst results of his life—and, oh, tweaking his oblique at one point for good measure. Rationalizing that his April served as his offseason, Herrera looked like his old self for the last couple weeks of the year. His contract assured he'd get another chance either way.

YEAR	TEAM	LVL	AGE	WHIP	ERA	DRA	WARP	MPH	FB%	WHF	CSP
2017	KCA	MLB	27	1.35	4.25	3.82	0.9	99.7	66.5	13.2	48.6
2018	KCA	MLB	28	0.82	1.05	3.88	0.3	99.0	64.9	15.7	48.3
2018	WAS	MLB	28	1.71	4.34	4.20	0.2	98.9	62.6	12.9	46.6
2019	CHA	MLB	29	1.62	6.14	5.21	0.1	98.3	55.9	13	47.1
2020	CHA	MLB	30	1.27	3.93	4.15	0.4	98.1	60.9	13.4	47.5

Kelvin Herrera, continued

Pitch Shape vs LHH

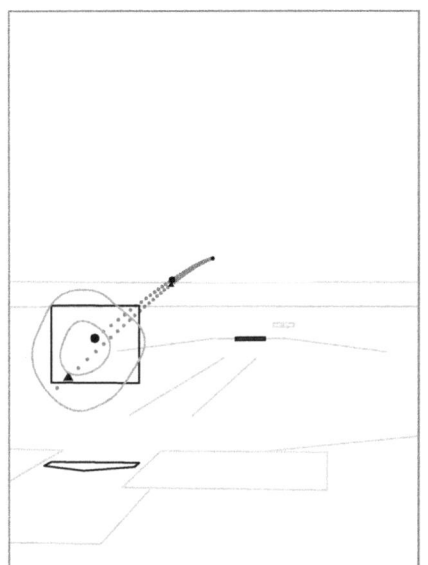

Pitch Shape vs RHH

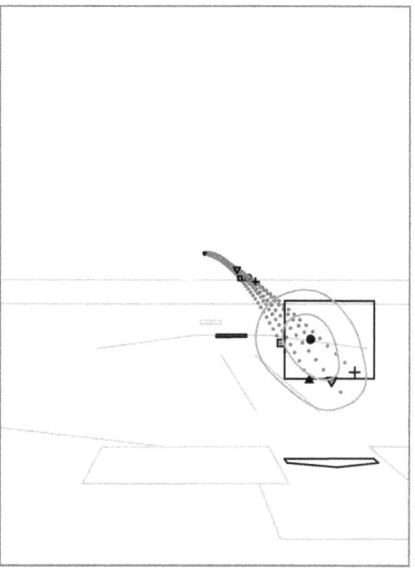

Type	Frequency	Velocity	H Movement	V Movement
● Fastball	49.8%	96.4 [111]	-6.1 [103]	-13.2 [107]
□ Sinker	6.1%	95.6 [116]	-9.9 [118]	-14.6 [120]
+ Cutter	10.9%	92.2 [122]	1.6 [99]	-19.1 [118]
▲ Changeup	19.3%	89 [113]	-11.6 [98]	-22.3 [115]
✕ Splitter				
▽ Slider	13.8%	82.6 [92]	11.4 [127]	-37.8 [86]
◇ Curveball				
⊕ Slow Curveball				
✱ Knuckleball				
▼ Screwball				

White Sox Player Analysis - 71

Chicago White Sox 2020

Dallas Keuchel LHP
Born: 01/01/88 Age: 32 Bats: L Throws: L
Height: 6'3" Weight: 205 Origin: Round 7, 2009 Draft (#221 overall)

YEAR	TEAM	LVL	AGE	W	L	SV	G	GS	IP	H	HR	BB/9	K/9	K	GB%	BABIP
2017	HOU	MLB	29	14	5	0	23	23	145²	116	15	2.9	7.7	125	68%	.256
2018	HOU	MLB	30	12	11	0	34	34	204²	211	18	2.6	6.7	153	55%	.300
2019	ROM	A	31	0	0	0	1	1	7	1	0	1.3	11.6	9	77%	.077
2019	MIS	AA	31	0	0	0	1	1	7	11	0	1.3	5.1	4	46%	.423
2019	ATL	MLB	31	8	8	0	19	19	112²	115	16	3.1	7.3	91	60%	.298
2020	CHA	MLB	32	12	8	0	29	29	172	169	22	3.0	7.0	133	58%	.285

Comparables: Chris Short, Wade Miley, Dillon Gee

On September 29, 2018, Keuchel threw his final pitch of that regular season. He wouldn't throw another regular season pitch until almost nine months later. Was there some sort of injury that ended up costing him a big chunk of 2019? Did he do something awful during the offseason sending him into baseball exile as part of his punishment? Well, sort of. He made the mistake of choosing to decline a qualifying offer and test the free agent waters. Even when the Braves finally signed him in June, he only agreed to a one-year deal. Despite the fact that he delivered more of the same production that we're used to seeing from him on the mound, his streak of three-win seasons ended at five. With a more normal offseason, Keuchel will look to start a new streak on the South Side in 2020.

YEAR	TEAM	LVL	AGE	WHIP	ERA	DRA	WARP	MPH	FB%	WHF	CSP
2017	HOU	MLB	29	1.12	2.90	3.64	3.1	90.8	68.2	12.3	38.9
2018	HOU	MLB	30	1.31	3.74	3.87	3.4	91.3	69.1	8.9	45
2019	ROM	A	31	0.29	0.00						
2019	MIS	AA	31	1.71	3.86	7.02	-0.2				
2019	ATL	MLB	31	1.37	3.75	4.25	1.9	89.9	74	9.5	40.8
2020	CHA	MLB	32	1.31	3.96	4.17	2.7	89.8	69.8	9.8	41.3

Dallas Keuchel, continued

Pitch Shape vs LHH

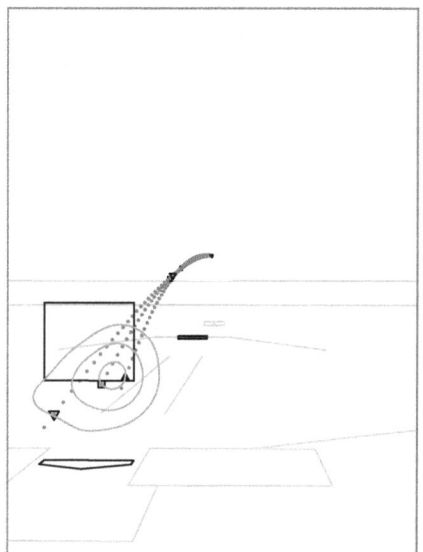

Pitch Shape vs RHH

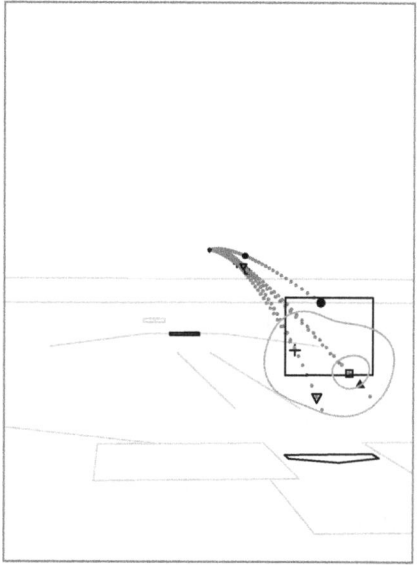

Type	Frequency	Velocity	H Movement	V Movement
● Fastball	4.9%	89.5 [92]	2.7 [118]	-18.5 [93]
☐ Sinker	48.9%	88.3 [78]	11.5 [108]	-26.6 [78]
+ Cutter	20.2%	86.2 [84]	-1.9 [100]	-25.9 [93]
▲ Changeup	14.5%	79.7 [80]	12.2 [95]	-34.9 [78]
✕ Splitter				
▽ Slider	11.4%	78.4 [75]	-6.8 [108]	-40.1 [80]
◇ Curveball				
✦ Slow Curveball				
✱ Knuckleball				
▼ Screwball				

Reynaldo López RHP

Born: 01/04/94 Age: 26 Bats: R Throws: R
Height: 6'1" Weight: 200 Origin: International Free Agent, 2012

YEAR	TEAM	LVL	AGE	W	L	SV	G	GS	IP	H	HR	BB/9	K/9	K	GB%	BABIP
2017	CHR	AAA	23	6	7	0	22	22	121	101	16	3.6	9.7	131	38%	.270
2017	CHA	MLB	23	3	3	0	8	8	47^2	49	7	2.6	5.7	30	30%	.271
2018	CHA	MLB	24	7	10	0	32	32	188^2	165	25	3.6	7.2	151	34%	.260
2019	CHA	MLB	25	10	15	0	33	33	184	203	35	3.2	8.3	169	35%	.316
2020	CHA	MLB	26	7	6	0	19	19	109	109	19	3.5	8.2	99	34%	.293

Comparables: Robert Gsellman, Tyler Mahle, Jake Faria

In a sense, López has made an absurd amount of progress in his development as a pitcher. It wasn't long ago he was a skinny Dominican 16-year-old who was not only without a professional contract, but catching for a lightly scouted youth team near San Pedro de Macorís. In another sense, his progress seems to have slackened in the past two years. He's continued to touch the upper-90s and pile up healthy innings despite his unusual looking delivery, yet has done little else to reward the White Sox's devotion to starting him. A team with less patience and more alternatives would have challenged him by now to throw as many 100 mph fastballs as he could out of the bullpen. The White Sox were rewarded for their unique patience by López's longtime teammate Lucas Giolito in 2019, but López will need a similarly stark turnaround to remain a starter past 2020. We think, anyway.

YEAR	TEAM	LVL	AGE	WHIP	ERA	DRA	WARP	MPH	FB%	WHF	CSP
2017	CHR	AAA	23	1.24	3.79	3.90	2.4				
2017	CHA	MLB	23	1.32	4.72	6.40	-0.4	97.8	60.9	9	48.8
2018	CHA	MLB	24	1.27	3.91	5.65	-0.7	98.2	60.9	10	49.2
2019	CHA	MLB	25	1.46	5.38	7.06	-2.6	98.2	58.6	12	51.2
2020	CHA	MLB	26	1.39	4.69	4.78	1.0	97.8	60.8	11.1	50.9

Reynaldo López, continued

Pitch Shape vs LHH	Pitch Shape vs RHH
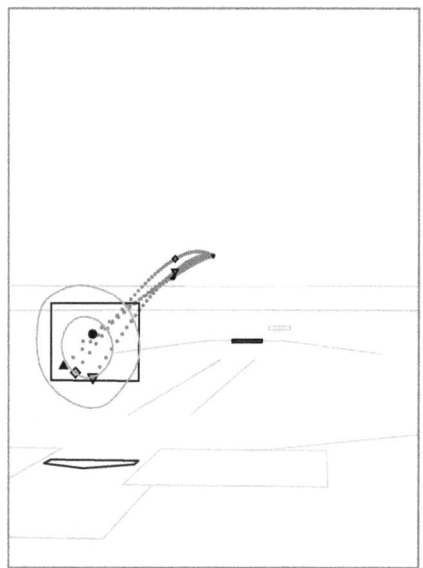	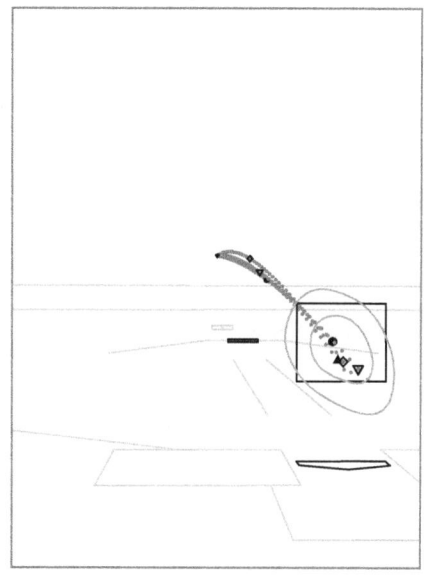

Type	Frequency	Velocity	H Movement	V Movement
● Fastball	58.5%	95.8 [110]	-8.5 [93]	-13.3 [107]
☐ Sinker				
+ Cutter				
▲ Changeup	14.8%	84.5 [97]	-9.9 [106]	-24.6 [108]
✕ Splitter				
▽ Slider	20.3%	84.3 [100]	3.6 [94]	-31.5 [105]
◇ Curveball	6.4%	78 [98]	3.3 [83]	-43.6 [108]
⊕ Slow Curveball				
✷ Knuckleball				
▼ Screwball				

Chicago White Sox 2020

Evan Marshall RHP

Born: 04/18/90 Age: 30 Bats: R Throws: R
Height: 6'2" Weight: 225 Origin: Round 4, 2011 Draft (#124 overall)

YEAR	TEAM	LVL	AGE	W	L	SV	G	GS	IP	H	HR	BB/9	K/9	K	GB%	BABIP
2017	TAC	AAA	27	1	0	1	13	1	21^2	28	4	2.9	10.8	26	61%	.400
2017	SEA	MLB	27	0	0	0	6	0	7^2	12	1	5.9	4.7	4	34%	.393
2018	COH	AAA	28	1	1	4	20	0	24	18	1	1.1	7.9	21	68%	.254
2018	CLE	MLB	28	0	0	0	10	0	7	12	0	5.1	11.6	9	56%	.522
2019	CHR	AAA	29	3	0	2	9	0	10	8	0	0.9	11.7	13	52%	.348
2019	CHA	MLB	29	4	2	0	55	0	50^2	42	5	4.3	7.3	41	52%	.266
2020	CHA	MLB	30	3	3	3	53	0	57	54	7	3.9	8.4	53	52%	.294

Comparables: Javy Guerra, Gregory Infante, JC Ramírez

Both before and after he exchanged texts with him—mostly discussing his "Forgetting Sarah Marshall"-themed Players' Weekend jersey—Marshall was clear about wanting actor Jason Segel to portray him in a movie about his life. There's certainly ample material for such a film, meaning it's a question of what tone the biopic would take. Maybe a more family-oriented movie would focus on Marshall's near-death experience after being struck by a line drive in 2015, and how the presence of his beloved pet dog roused him from a coma. An Oscar-bait type of approach would focus more on the draining grind to find a big-league home Marshall has faced over the last four seasons, as sympathy for his suffering gave way to scrutiny at his ability to match his pre-injury form, until he remade himself as a yeoman-like weak contact-hunting sinkerballer in an age of riding four-seam strikeout artists. Or they could make a divisive, dark-toned film loved only by movie snobs who appreciate the ambiguous ending where below-average peripheral stats suggest that trouble is always lurking around the corner for Marshall, even after successful year in the White Sox bullpen.

YEAR	TEAM	LVL	AGE	WHIP	ERA	DRA	WARP	MPH	FB%	WHF	CSP
2017	TAC	AAA	27	1.62	4.15	5.56	-0.1				
2017	SEA	MLB	27	2.22	9.39	8.07	-0.2	95.7	65.6	7.4	46.6
2018	COH	AAA	28	0.88	1.12	2.78	0.6				
2018	CLE	MLB	28	2.29	7.71	3.65	0.1	95.5	54.7	17.3	43.1
2019	CHR	AAA	29	0.90	0.00	2.28	0.4				
2019	CHA	MLB	29	1.30	2.49	5.08	0.2	95.2	43.9	11.7	40.1
2020	CHA	MLB	30	1.38	4.19	4.33	0.5	94.5	46.5	12.1	42.6

Evan Marshall, continued

Pitch Shape vs LHH

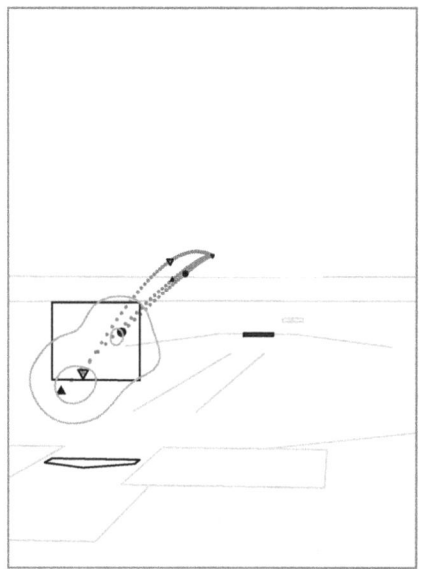

Pitch Shape vs RHH

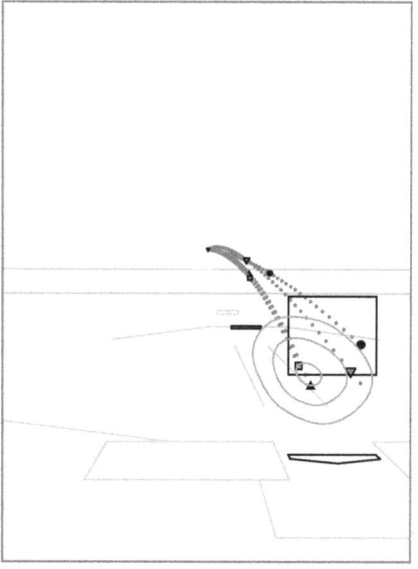

Type	Frequency	Velocity	H Movement	V Movement
● Fastball	23.4%	93.9 [104]	-9 [90]	-15.5 [101]
□ Sinker	20.5%	93.7 [106]	-14.1 [91]	-21.3 [97]
+ Cutter				
▲ Changeup	39.4%	87.8 [109]	-13 [92]	-30.3 [92]
✕ Splitter				
▽ Slider	16.7%	83.3 [95]	8 [112]	-42.4 [73]
◇ Curveball				
✦ Slow Curveball				
✳ Knuckleball				
▼ Screwball				

Chicago White Sox 2020

Adalberto Mejía LHP
Born: 06/20/93   Age: 27   Bats: R   Throws: L
Height: 6'3"   Weight: 195   Origin: International Free Agent, 2011

YEAR	TEAM	LVL	AGE	W	L	SV	G	GS	IP	H	HR	BB/9	K/9	K	GB%	BABIP
2017	ROC	AAA	24	1	1	0	6	6	28²	26	1	1.9	6.9	22	51%	.294
2017	MIN	MLB	24	4	7	0	21	21	98	110	13	4.0	7.8	85	41%	.328
2018	ROC	AAA	25	5	3	0	15	12	63¹	55	3	2.8	8.8	62	43%	.294
2018	MIN	MLB	25	2	0	0	5	4	22¹	17	1	3.6	5.2	13	40%	.239
2019	LAA	MLB	26	0	0	0	20	0	13	9	1	5.5	9.0	13	39%	.229
2019	SLN	MLB	26	0	0	0	2	0	3	8	0	3.0	6.0	2	14%	.571
2019	MIN	MLB	26	0	2	0	13	0	15¹	16	3	7.0	8.8	15	25%	.317
2020	LAA	MLB	27	1	1	0	12	0	12	12	2	3.7	7.6	10	36%	.290

Comparables: Jeff Hoffman, Felix Doubront, Robert Stephenson

The word "odyssey" conjures something cool and epic, but Mejía's 2019 voyage was something far less than an excellent adventure. DFAed by Minnesota after a rocky start to the season, he was claimed and quickly DFAed again by the Angels, picked up by the Cards, jettisoned shortly thereafter, and once again grabbed by the Halos, only to be outrighted to Triple-A in August. It's not that anything has drastically changed in Mejía's skills, but the talent was fringy to begin with, and while the future seems a bit hazy at the moment, the lefty should find himself stopping periodically in major-league ports of call.

YEAR	TEAM	LVL	AGE	WHIP	ERA	DRA	WARP	MPH	FB%	WHF	CSP
2017	ROC	AAA	24	1.12	2.83	3.92	0.6				
2017	MIN	MLB	24	1.57	4.50	6.02	-0.5	94.4	56.3	11.2	43.6
2018	ROC	AAA	25	1.18	3.27	3.68	1.3				
2018	MIN	MLB	25	1.16	2.01	6.86	-0.4	95.0	59.1	9.5	48
2019	LAA	MLB	26	1.31	3.46	8.44	-0.4	94.8	55.4	11.9	46.4
2019	SLN	MLB	26	3.00	9.00	6.56	0.0	93.6	61.8	5.9	54.3
2019	MIN	MLB	26	1.83	8.80	8.19	-0.5	96.0	51	10.6	42.6
2020	LAA	MLB	27	1.40	4.49	4.58	0.1	94.3	56.6	10.9	46.4

Adalberto Mejía, continued

Pitch Shape vs LHH

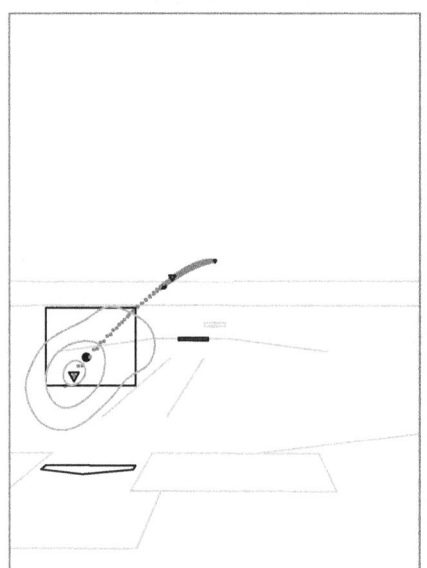

Pitch Shape vs RHH

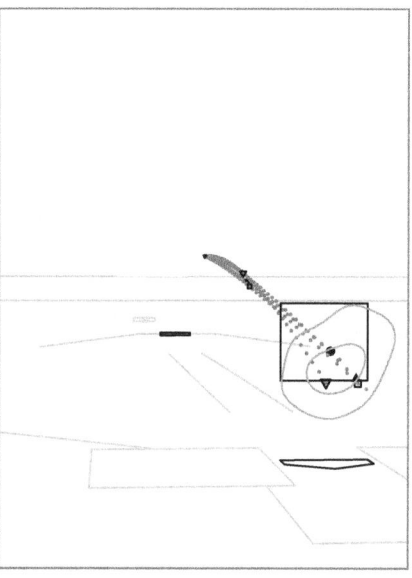

Type	Frequency	Velocity	H Movement	V Movement
● Fastball	44.2%	93.3 [103]	7.7 [96]	-15 [103]
☐ Sinker	9.7%	92.2 [98]	13.8 [93]	-21.6 [96]
+ Cutter				
▲ Changeup	16.4%	81.8 [87]	13.6 [88]	-31.1 [89]
✕ Splitter				
▽ Slider	28.9%	84.8 [102]	-2.6 [90]	-31.9 [103]
◇ Curveball				
✦ Slow Curveball				
✱ Knuckleball				
▼ Screwball				

Carlos Rodón   LHP
Born: 12/10/92   Age: 27   Bats: L   Throws: L
Height: 6'3"   Weight: 235   Origin: Round 1, 2014 Draft (#3 overall)

YEAR	TEAM	LVL	AGE	W	L	SV	G	GS	IP	H	HR	BB/9	K/9	K	GB%	BABIP
2017	CHR	AAA	24	0	3	0	3	3	13²	17	0	4.6	7.2	11	50%	.354
2017	CHA	MLB	24	2	5	0	12	12	69¹	64	12	4.0	9.9	76	45%	.297
2018	CHR	AAA	25	1	0	0	3	3	12²	10	0	3.6	15.6	22	56%	.435
2018	CHA	MLB	25	6	8	0	20	20	120²	97	15	4.1	6.7	90	42%	.243
2019	CHA	MLB	26	3	2	0	7	7	34²	33	4	4.4	11.9	46	43%	.322
2020	CHA	MLB	27	2	2	0	21	5	39	35	6	4.0	9.2	39	39%	.276

Comparables: Daniel Norris, Eduardo Rodriguez, Henry Owens

Rodón finally had a healthy (and full) spring training for the first time in years, which simultaneously seems like: 1) an irrelevant trifle and 2) a reason to vault his strikeout rate up 10 percentage points. His career has been frustrating but he's too talented to do anything but let it play out.

His strikeout rate actually vaulted by 11.5 percentage points despite a precipitous loss of velocity. He compensated for that loss by throwing just *so* many more sliders. Maybe it means he's not healthy, but his is an elite slider and if Patrick Corbin can do it, why not Rodón?

So it turns out Rodón was *definitely* not healthy, and he will be churning through Tommy John rehab instead of enjoying a healthy and full 2020 spring training. It is not good to tear a UCL, but perhaps it explains the precipitous velocity loss and certainly would explain getting torched by the dang Tigers and Orioles in his last two starts.

Maybe at some point he'll encounter all three—being healthy, flipping that nasty slider a ton, and throwing hard again—at the same time. Why not? His career has been frustrating but he's too talented to do anything but let it play out.

YEAR	TEAM	LVL	AGE	WHIP	ERA	DRA	WARP	MPH	FB%	WHF	CSP
2017	CHR	AAA	24	1.76	9.22	6.53	-0.1				
2017	CHA	MLB	24	1.37	4.15	5.13	0.3	96.6	61.2	11.1	47.9
2018	CHR	AAA	25	1.18	1.42	3.18	0.3				
2018	CHA	MLB	25	1.26	4.18	6.57	-1.8	96.1	59.8	9.7	47.6
2019	CHA	MLB	26	1.44	5.19	4.05	0.6	94.7	51.9	13.1	46.8
2020	CHA	MLB	27	1.34	4.30	4.41	0.4	95.5	59	10.9	47.9

Carlos Rodón, continued

Pitch Shape vs LHH

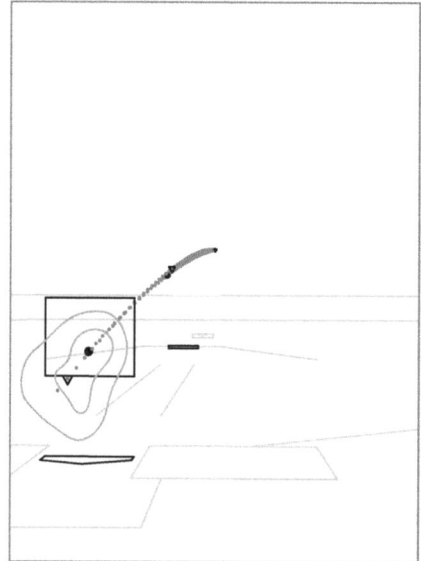

Pitch Shape vs RHH

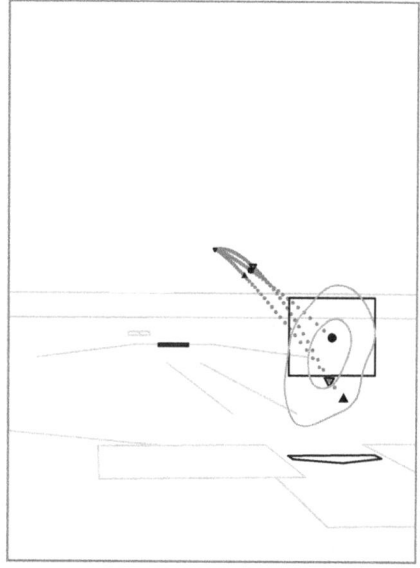

Type	Frequency	Velocity	H Movement	V Movement
● Fastball	51.9%	92.1 [99]	7.5 [97]	-14.9 [103]
☐ Sinker				
+ Cutter				
▲ Changeup	10.8%	84.7 [98]	13.9 [87]	-27.5 [100]
✕ Splitter				
▽ Slider	37.4%	84.3 [100]	-5.5 [102]	-35 [95]
◇ Curveball				
⊕ Slow Curveball				
✱ Knuckleball				
▼ Screwball				

Chicago White Sox 2020

José Ruiz RHP
Born: 10/21/94 Age: 25 Bats: R Throws: R
Height: 6'1" Weight: 190 Origin: International Free Agent, 2011

YEAR	TEAM	LVL	AGE	W	L	SV	G	GS	IP	H	HR	BB/9	K/9	K	GB%	BABIP
2017	LEL	A+	22	1	2	2	44	0	49²	57	7	4.5	8.2	45	33%	.345
2017	SDN	MLB	22	0	0	0	1	0	1	0	0	9.0	9.0	1	50%	.000
2018	WNS	A+	23	0	0	2	10	0	13¹	6	2	3.4	14.9	22	33%	.182
2018	BIR	AA	23	3	1	14	33	0	45¹	33	2	3.8	10.9	55	41%	.290
2018	CHA	MLB	23	0	0	0	6	0	4¹	5	1	6.2	12.5	6	42%	.364
2019	CHR	AAA	24	0	0	7	11	0	14¹	9	0	4.4	9.4	15	34%	.257
2019	CHA	MLB	24	1	4	0	40	1	40	56	6	5.4	7.9	35	37%	.377
2020	CHA	MLB	25	1	1	0	16	0	17	17	3	4.4	8.1	15	37%	.288

Comparables: Ian Gibaut, Shawn Armstrong, Jaye Chapman

Ruiz was optioned six times during the course of last season, and averaged fewer than three innings per assignment before being rocketed back to the majors. For a converted ex-catcher who throws hard and does little else well, the White Sox's scattershot usage of him seems telling. Most good relievers have been treated as if they were functionally worthless for some stretch of their career, yet Ruiz will require a quantum leap of development—not unlike going from light-hitting A-ball catcher to the ninth-best reliever in a bad bullpen—if he's going to achieve a reoccurring presence in this book.

YEAR	TEAM	LVL	AGE	WHIP	ERA	DRA	WARP	MPH	FB%	WHF	CSP
2017	LEL	A+	22	1.65	5.98	5.93	-0.6				
2017	SDN	MLB	22	1.00	0.00	9.17	0.0	96.6	80	6.7	49.2
2018	WNS	A+	23	0.82	2.70	2.36	0.4				
2018	BIR	AA	23	1.15	3.18	3.37	0.8				
2018	CHA	MLB	23	1.85	4.15	2.40	0.1	98.0	58.4	16.9	44.7
2019	CHR	AAA	24	1.12	1.26	2.50	0.5				
2019	CHA	MLB	24	2.00	5.62	8.13	-1.2	98.8	61.6	12	47.3
2020	CHA	MLB	25	1.47	4.94	4.94	0.0	98.4	63	12.6	48

José Ruiz, continued

Pitch Shape vs LHH

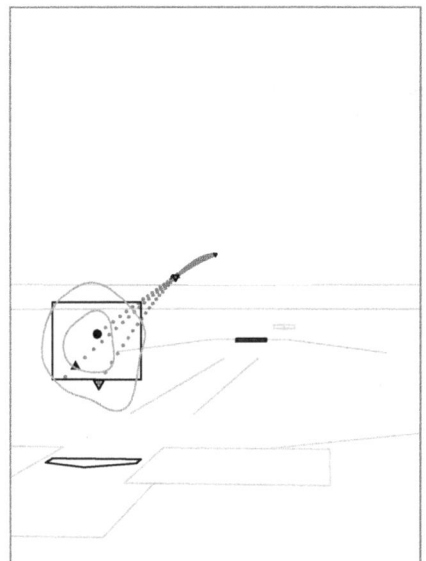

Pitch Shape vs RHH

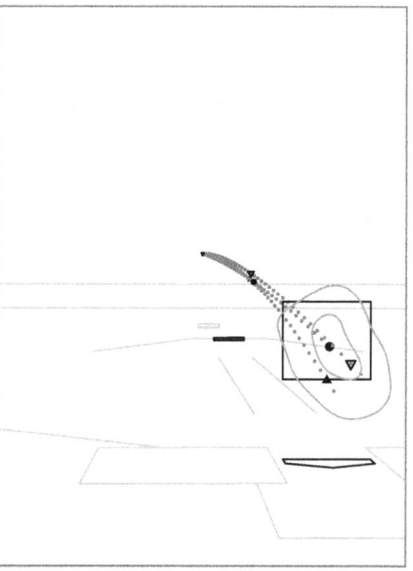

Type	Frequency	Velocity	H Movement	V Movement
● Fastball	61.6%	96.7 [112]	-3.9 [113]	-10.5 [114]
☐ Sinker				
+ Cutter				
▲ Changeup	13.0%	87.1 [107]	-10.5 [103]	-24 [110]
✕ Splitter				
▽ Slider	24.9%	88.4 [117]	4.2 [97]	-28.1 [114]
◇ Curveball				
⊕ Slow Curveball				
✳ Knuckleball				
▼ Screwball				

White Sox Player Analysis

PLAYER COMMENTS WITHOUT GRAPHS

Luis Alexander Basabe OF
Born: 08/26/96 Age: 23 Bats: B Throws: R
Height: 6'0" Weight: 160 Origin: International Free Agent, 2012

YEAR	TEAM	LVL	AGE	PA	R	2B	3B	HR	RBI	BB	K	SB	CS	AVG/OBP/SLG
2017	WNS	A+	20	435	52	12	5	5	36	49	104	17	6	.221/.320/.320
2018	WNS	A+	21	245	36	12	5	9	30	34	64	7	8	.266/.370/.502
2018	BIR	AA	21	270	41	9	3	6	26	30	76	9	4	.251/.340/.394
2019	BIR	AA	22	291	31	12	1	3	30	29	85	9	4	.246/.324/.336
2020	CHA	MLB	23	105	11	4	1	3	12	9	35	2	1	.217/.286/.370

Comparables: Daniel Fields, Lewis Brinson, Jeimer Candelario

Basabe already invoked the "bad due to injury" provision in 2017, before rebounding with a Carolina League All-Star and Futures Game appearance in 2018 after offseason knee surgery. When he broke his right hamate bone in February, most hope of any kind of normal season went out the door. Sure enough, the power that lifts Basabe's profile onto the level of a potential everyday player was absent for most of 2019. Between that and a pair of quad strains, his most impressive accomplishment was managing to not have his game go significantly backward. Basabe is still just 23 years old, so treading water in Double-A is not the worst place to be. Alas, the smooth path he needed to transcend a fourth-outfielder destiny does not seem in the stars.

YEAR	TEAM	LVL	AGE	PA	DRC+	VORP	BABIP	BRR	FRAA	WARP
2017	WNS	A+	20	435	85	9.6	.292	4.4	CF(92): 0.1, RF(12): -0.4	1.1
2018	WNS	A+	21	245	144	19.7	.341	-2.0	CF(28): 2.2, LF(16): 1.5	2.0
2018	BIR	AA	21	270	108	13.3	.344	2.1	CF(42): -1.9, RF(15): 0.3	1.1
2019	BIR	AA	22	291	92	3.3	.355	1.4	CF(25): 0.3, LF(22): -2.7	0.6
2020	CHA	MLB	23	105	73	-0.3	.307	0.2	LF 0, CF 0	0.0

Luis González OF

Born: 09/10/95 Age: 24 Bats: L Throws: L
Height: 6'1" Weight: 195 Origin: Round 3, 2017 Draft (#87 overall)

YEAR	TEAM	LVL	AGE	PA	R	2B	3B	HR	RBI	BB	K	SB	CS	AVG/OBP/SLG
2017	KAN	A	21	277	26	13	4	2	12	38	50	2	3	.245/.356/.361
2018	KAN	A	22	255	35	16	2	8	26	21	57	7	2	.300/.358/.491
2018	WNS	A+	22	288	50	24	3	6	45	27	46	3	5	.313/.376/.504
2019	BIR	AA	23	535	63	18	4	9	59	47	89	17	9	.247/.316/.359
2020	CHA	MLB	24	251	24	12	1	6	27	18	57	1	1	.234/.293/.380

Comparables: Gary Brown, Danny Ortiz, Lane Adams

González hasn't so much as dominated a Google search of his own name since he started playing baseball. But not dominating Double-A will put the 24-year-old González on a time crunch, as the first taste of Southern League pitching is often a separating year for mid-tier position prospects. His tweener profile prompts a lot of questions about his future home and utility if there aren't shiny numbers sitting next to it at all times. (Can he stick in center or can he hit enough to play right? Does he have enough pop despite his lack of size? Does his open stance give up too much of the outer half while enabling pull-side pop?) There's probably a future big-leaguer in some fashion in there, but you'll have to get more specific in your search bar entry if you want to get more details on him than that.

YEAR	TEAM	LVL	AGE	PA	DRC+	VORP	BABIP	BRR	FRAA	WARP
2017	KAN	A	21	277	116	10.9	.302	-0.2	CF(31): -2.9, LF(18): -0.1	0.8
2018	KAN	A	22	255	147	19.8	.365	-0.6	CF(39): -1.0, RF(13): -1.9	1.6
2018	WNS	A+	22	288	150	26.8	.354	5.8	CF(31): 3.9, LF(14): 0.2	3.1
2019	BIR	AA	23	535	103	13.0	.281	1.0	CF(60): 0.7, RF(29): 1.1	2.1
2020	CHA	MLB	24	251	78	0.7	.284	-0.3	CF 1, RF 0	0.3

Chicago White Sox 2020

Nick Madrigal 2B

Born: 03/05/97 Age: 23 Bats: R Throws: R
Height: 5'7" Weight: 165 Origin: Round 1, 2018 Draft (#4 overall)

YEAR	TEAM	LVL	AGE	PA	R	2B	3B	HR	RBI	BB	K	SB	CS	AVG/OBP/SLG
2018	KAN	A	21	49	9	3	0	0	6	1	0	2	2	.341/.347/.409
2018	WNS	A+	21	107	14	4	0	0	9	5	5	6	3	.306/.355/.347
2019	WNS	A+	22	218	20	10	2	2	27	17	6	17	4	.272/.346/.377
2019	BIR	AA	22	180	30	11	2	1	16	14	5	14	6	.341/.400/.451
2019	CHR	AAA	22	134	26	6	1	1	12	13	5	4	3	.331/.398/.424
2020	CHA	MLB	23	420	39	20	1	6	38	26	29	12	6	.259/.315/.359

Comparables: Kevin Newman, Dixon Machado, Steve Clevenger

For the plurality of the season, Madrigal was in the Carolina League. He ran extremely hard, made lightning quick transfers and, due to a lack of power, was not much better than the average hitter playing High-A baseball on the east coast—that despite possessing insanely distinct contact skills. From there on out, he hit .337/.399/.440 while playing the rest of the season at two higher levels. That's an overtly more impressive testament to Madrigal's abilities, but really a more extreme form of what had already been demonstrated. He unleashes blizzards of singles that look like BABIP-fueled hot streaks until they stretch on for months and seasons rather than weeks. His well-rounded game full of up-the-middle defense and plus running raises the floor around his offense, and his biggest advocates tout that there's more ability to drive the ball with authority than the simple numbers game of putting every single ball in play would immediately indicate. He's one of the oddest prospects in the game, and therefore one of the most interesting.

YEAR	TEAM	LVL	AGE	PA	DRC+	VORP	BABIP	BRR	FRAA	WARP
2018	KAN	A	21	49	145	5.3	.319	1.1	2B(12): 0.9	0.6
2018	WNS	A+	21	107	121	2.7	.319	0.0	2B(25): -1.8	0.3
2019	WNS	A+	22	218	114	11.5	.269	3.6	2B(41): 3.4	1.6
2019	BIR	AA	22	180	154	14.0	.348	0.3	2B(39): 0.1	1.6
2019	CHR	AAA	22	134	103	6.0	.336	0.5	2B(27): 1.5	0.6
2020	CHA	MLB	23	420	83	7.9	.268	0.2	2B 2	1.0

Daniel Palka   RF

Born: 10/28/91   Age: 28   Bats: L   Throws: L
Height: 6'2"   Weight: 220   Origin: Round 3, 2013 Draft (#88 overall)

YEAR	TEAM	LVL	AGE	PA	R	2B	3B	HR	RBI	BB	K	SB	CS	AVG/OBP/SLG
2017	ROC	AAA	25	362	47	13	3	11	42	27	80	1	2	.274/.329/.431
2018	CHR	AAA	26	73	11	3	0	3	7	10	21	1	2	.286/.384/.476
2018	CHA	MLB	26	449	56	15	3	27	67	30	153	2	1	.240/.294/.484
2019	CHR	AAA	27	471	83	23	0	27	72	72	109	2	0	.263/.374/.527
2019	CHA	MLB	27	93	4	0	0	2	4	8	35	0	1	.107/.194/.179
2020	CHA	MLB	28	251	31	9	1	14	37	24	83	3	1	.220/.298/.446

Comparables: Tyler Austin, Jonny Gomes, Jerry Sands

There's never a good situation for a major-league player to forget how to hit, but it's probably significantly more inconvenient for a lumbering...er, lumberjack-type build slugger like Palka. Possessing no true defensive home (and quickly contributing negative defensive value at any spot he lays his hat), an 0-for-32 slump to start the year sent him from Opening Day right fielder to playing right field in Charlotte within the first month of the season. Either comfortably or confoundingly or both, Palka retained the ability to produce offensively in Triple-A, where he was exiled for most of 2019. He'll probably do the same in 2020, when he'll be a 28-year-old platoon bat who has suddenly cast a lot more doubt on how reliable that description remains.

YEAR	TEAM	LVL	AGE	PA	DRC+	VORP	BABIP	BRR	FRAA	WARP
2017	ROC	AAA	25	362	105	9.4	.329	1.2	RF(61): 3.5, LF(25): 0.1	1.3
2018	CHR	AAA	26	73	123	3.7	.385	0.1	RF(15): 0.5	0.4
2018	CHA	MLB	26	449	100	11.4	.308	-0.8	RF(43): -3.0, LF(26): -0.5	0.4
2019	CHR	AAA	27	471	124	9.9	.293	-6.1	RF(62): -5.9, 1B(13): -0.4	0.9
2019	CHA	MLB	27	93	50	-4.0	.149	0.1	RF(23): -4.0, 1B(1): -0.1	-0.8
2020	CHA	MLB	28	251	88	4.2	.279	-0.2	RF -2, LF -1	0.1

Chicago White Sox 2020

Luis Robert CF
Born: 08/03/97 Age: 22 Bats: R Throws: R
Height: 6'3" Weight: 185 Origin: International Free Agent, 2017

YEAR	TEAM	LVL	AGE	PA	R	2B	3B	HR	RBI	BB	K	SB	CS	AVG/OBP/SLG
2017	DWS	RK	19	114	17	8	1	3	14	22	23	12	3	.310/.491/.536
2018	KAN	A	20	50	5	3	1	0	4	4	12	4	2	.289/.360/.400
2018	WNS	A+	20	140	21	6	1	0	11	8	37	8	2	.244/.317/.309
2019	WNS	A+	21	84	21	5	3	8	24	4	20	8	2	.453/.512/.920
2019	BIR	AA	21	244	43	16	3	8	29	13	54	21	6	.314/.362/.518
2019	CHR	AAA	21	223	44	10	5	16	39	11	55	7	3	.297/.341/.634
2020	CHA	MLB	22	595	74	30	4	29	86	30	175	18	6	.262/.315/.487

Comparables: Brett Phillips, Lewis Brinson, Greg Golson

Robert's plate discipline and offensive performance dipped precipitously with every promotion during his three-level dash through the minors in 2019, to the point where he was striking out five times as often as he took a free pass in Triple-A. (That stint in Charlotte also saw him launch 16 home runs in 47 games, which is a pretty metal, even in the rarified mania that was 2019 Triple-A baseball.) Robert was sold as an impossibly physically gifted toolshed who dominated the best professional competition in Cuba at a young age, and finally healthy in 2019, a 30-30 (and more) season displayed all the physical gifts. As for the level of polish in his game, there's likely a myriad of approach adjustments he will need in the majors, but those clearly aren't going to be forced at any level of competition below that. Where he ultimately falls between world-conquering stardom and limitlessly talented but somewhat frustrating regular contributor will get hashed out sometime over the next decade.

YEAR	TEAM	LVL	AGE	PA	DRC+	VORP	BABIP	BRR	FRAA	WARP
2017	DWS	RK	19	114	203	20.6	.397	2.5	CF(19): -0.5	1.7
2018	KAN	A	20	50	105	3.0	.394	-0.2	CF(10): 0.0	0.1
2018	WNS	A+	20	140	83	2.7	.341	0.5	CF(27): 3.1, RF(4): -0.4	0.5
2019	WNS	A+	21	84	273	18.3	.553	-1.2	CF(13): 1.9	1.6
2019	BIR	AA	21	244	128	20.2	.384	2.5	CF(36): 1.9, RF(7): -0.8	1.8
2019	CHR	AAA	21	223	114	13.2	.324	1.2	CF(46): 6.5	1.7
2020	CHA	MLB	22	595	109	28.6	.333	1.9	CF 8, RF 0	3.8

Blake Rutherford OF

Born: 05/02/97 Age: 23 Bats: L Throws: R
Height: 6'2" Weight: 210 Origin: Round 1, 2016 Draft (#18 overall)

YEAR	TEAM	LVL	AGE	PA	R	2B	3B	HR	RBI	BB	K	SB	CS	AVG/OBP/SLG
2017	CSC	A	20	304	41	20	2	2	30	25	55	9	4	.281/.342/.391
2017	KAN	A	20	136	11	5	0	0	5	13	21	1	0	.213/.289/.254
2018	WNS	A+	21	487	67	25	9	7	78	34	90	15	8	.293/.345/.436
2019	BIR	AA	22	480	50	17	3	7	49	37	118	9	2	.265/.319/.365
2020	CHA	MLB	23	251	23	11	1	5	25	16	72	3	1	.237/.289/.363

Comparables: Destin Hood, Sócrates Brito, Eddie Rosario

YOU, UNFEELING MONSTER WHO REVELS IN THE PAIN OF OTHERS: Rutherford is a future corner guy whose polish was supposed to carry a profile that lacks standout tools, specifically the typical impact power of a corner outfielder, and the speed that would make sticking in center field or adding a ton of value on defense realistic. As for that polish, he has hit .280/.337/.400 in four professional seasons, with the most damage coming when he was in rookie ball. There's just not much reason to expect a big-league regular if you didn't see one already.

US, SHAMELESS OPTIMISTS: Rutherford will be 22 on Opening Day with time yet to show more pitch recognition and ability to adjust, has pretty much not played against competition that was his same age since rookie ball, and just flashed standout contact ability during a strong finish to an otherwise nightmarish 2019 season. Surely not *every* team that put first-round grades on him out of high school were suffering from madness.

YEAR	TEAM	LVL	AGE	PA	DRC+	VORP	BABIP	BRR	FRAA	WARP
2017	CSC	A	20	304	98	10.8	.341	-2.6	CF(39): -5.6, LF(13): -0.5	-0.3
2017	KAN	A	20	136	98	-4.9	.257	-0.1	CF(13): -1.3, LF(10): -0.3	0.1
2018	WNS	A+	21	487	121	18.7	.351	1.1	RF(74): -2.5, LF(15): -2.7	1.4
2019	BIR	AA	22	480	95	7.1	.343	2.4	RF(67): 1.7, LF(29): -1.7	1.0
2020	CHA	MLB	23	251	74	-0.5	.318	-0.1	RF -1, LF -1	-0.5

Chicago White Sox 2020

Gavin Sheets 1B

Born: 04/23/96 Age: 24 Bats: L Throws: L
Height: 6'4" Weight: 230 Origin: Round 2, 2017 Draft (#49 overall)

YEAR	TEAM	LVL	AGE	PA	R	2B	3B	HR	RBI	BB	K	SB	CS	AVG/OBP/SLG
2017	KAN	A	21	218	16	10	0	3	25	20	34	0	0	.266/.346/.365
2018	WNS	A+	22	497	58	28	2	6	61	52	81	1	0	.293/.368/.407
2019	BIR	AA	23	527	56	18	1	16	83	54	99	3	1	.267/.345/.414
2020	CHA	MLB	24	251	26	12	0	8	29	20	58	0	0	.249/.314/.402

Comparables: Russ Canzler, Matt Thaiss, David Cooper

Tasked with the solemn task of cranking more rocking dingers as a complement to his admirable contact and plate discipline, Sheets recovered from an ugly start in Double-A to fulfill his central purpose. His 16 homers were top-10 in the category in the pitching-friendly Southern League, even if everyone ahead of him among the league leaders did it in fewer than his 527 plate appearances in Birmingham. That continued a trend for him, as he's never pushed aside all the doubts about his game—he's a bat-only prospect without an elite bat—by laying waste to opposing pitching. Sheets will almost surely play in the Show, but it's unclear for how long.

YEAR	TEAM	LVL	AGE	PA	DRC+	VORP	BABIP	BRR	FRAA	WARP
2017	KAN	A	21	218	112	2.1	.308	-2.4	1B(50): -2.1	0.0
2018	WNS	A+	22	497	134	10.5	.344	-3.9	1B(108): -4.3	1.4
2019	BIR	AA	23	527	129	10.4	.305	-6.3	1B(109): 3.8	1.9
2020	CHA	MLB	24	251	90	4.2	.303	-0.5	1B 0	0.5

Andrew Vaughn 1B

Born: 04/03/98 Age: 22 Bats: R Throws: R
Height: 6'0" Weight: 214 Origin: Round 1, 2019 Draft (#3 overall)

YEAR	TEAM	LVL	AGE	PA	R	2B	3B	HR	RBI	BB	K	SB	CS	AVG/OBP/SLG
2019	KAN	A	21	103	14	7	0	2	11	14	18	0	0	.253/.388/.410
2019	WNS	A+	21	126	16	8	0	3	21	16	17	0	1	.252/.349/.411
2020	CHA	MLB	22	251	24	12	0	6	26	19	56	3	1	.222/.294/.360

Comparables: Ty France, Mike Ford, Patrick Wisdom

In the rare instances where Vaughn rolls over a ball and chops a slow roller to third base, it's hard not to think of *Star Wars* as he digs in to beat out the throw. Specifically, it's that scene in *The Empire Strikes Back* where Han Solo pulls the handle for the hyperdrive, expecting the stars to streak in the sky as his ship leaps into light speed, only for the engine to whine as the Millenium Falcon keeps chugging along at the same unsuitable pace. Vaughn has a throwing arm strong enough that he was recruited out of high school as a two-way player and dutifully works on his glove. But, in general, there's not the oozing athleticism present to provide some extra value to his game outside his bat. That, in the end, could just be another compliment for his truly exceptional bat: plus power to all-fields as well as a plate approach so disciplined that every at-bat takes on the feeling that the opposing pitcher is being audited after three years of not self-paying taxes on his freelance income. This is as advanced and polished as a young hitter gets—it's a good thing, too, because there's not a fallback option if flaws emerge.

YEAR	TEAM	LVL	AGE	PA	DRC+	VORP	BABIP	BRR	FRAA	WARP
2019	KAN	A	21	103	137	6.0	.297	1.2	1B(19): -0.5	0.6
2019	WNS	A+	21	126	140	6.0	.270	-0.3	1B(15): -0.3	0.5
2020	CHA	MLB	22	251	76	0.2	.270	0.0	1B -2	-0.2

Seby Zavala C

Born: 08/28/93 Age: 26 Bats: R Throws: R
Height: 5'11" Weight: 215 Origin: Round 12, 2015 Draft (#352 overall)

YEAR	TEAM	LVL	AGE	PA	R	2B	3B	HR	RBI	BB	K	SB	CS	AVG/OBP/SLG
2017	KAN	A	23	207	32	8	0	13	34	13	52	0	0	.259/.327/.514
2017	WNS	A+	23	228	31	13	0	8	38	24	52	1	0	.302/.376/.485
2018	BIR	AA	24	232	32	7	0	11	31	27	65	0	0	.271/.358/.472
2018	CHR	AAA	24	191	18	15	0	2	20	6	44	0	2	.243/.267/.359
2019	CHR	AAA	25	331	49	14	0	20	45	26	116	1	1	.222/.296/.471
2019	CHA	MLB	25	12	1	0	0	0	0	0	9	0	0	.083/.083/.083
2020	CHA	MLB	26	251	22	9	0	7	26	16	97	0	0	.191/.252/.328

Comparables: Cameron Rupp, Adam Engel, JaCoby Jones

Your defensive-minded, game-managing catching prospect clubbing 20 home runs in Triple-A just isn't the coup it was before the top levels of professional baseball started using glorified racquetballs in games. The gritty and weathered Zavala has overcome waiting until the third day of the draft to hear his name called and a wealth of nagging injuries to get to this point. He posted the highest home-run total and second-highest ISO of his professional career at Charlotte in 2019, but looked overmatched and overwhelmed against big-league pitching during two cups of coffee in Chicago. With decent power production being easier to find than ever, and the White Sox more interested in squeezing offense from the catching position than most, the White Sox might end up saying bye to Seby.

YEAR	TEAM	P. COUNT	FRM RUNS	BLK RUNS	THRW RUNS	TOT RUNS
2018	BIR	4264	3.3	0.1	0.4	4.0
2018	CHR	4728	-2.6	0.0	-0.1	-2.3
2019	CHA	345	0.1	0.1	0.0	0.2
2019	CHR	7180	5.4	-0.1	0.4	5.6
2020	CHA	8438	2.8	1.2	-0.3	3.6

YEAR	TEAM	LVL	AGE	PA	DRC+	VORP	BABIP	BRR	FRAA	WARP
2017	KAN	A	23	207	133	17.2	.289	0.9	C(43): -1.5	1.5
2017	WNS	A+	23	228	141	20.1	.373	3.0	C(34): 0.9	2.1
2018	BIR	AA	24	232	133	18.4	.339	0.0	C(31): 4.0	2.0
2018	CHR	AAA	24	191	81	-2.6	.304	-1.2	C(35): -3.0	-0.1
2019	CHR	AAA	25	331	78	-3.2	.282	-1.7	C(52): 6.8, 1B(18): -0.3	0.7
2019	CHA	MLB	25	12	52	-0.1	.333	0.0	C(3): 0.2	0.0
2020	CHA	MLB	26	251	52	-8.1	.289	-0.5	C 4, 1B 0	-0.4

Bernardo Flores LHP

Born: 08/23/95   Age: 24   Bats: L   Throws: L
Height: 6'2"   Weight: 190   Origin: Round 7, 2016 Draft (#206 overall)

YEAR	TEAM	LVL	AGE	W	L	SV	G	GS	IP	H	HR	BB/9	K/9	K	GB%	BABIP
2017	KAN	A	21	8	4	0	14	14	78	73	5	1.5	8.1	70	50%	.308
2017	WNS	A+	21	2	3	0	9	9	40^1	43	5	4.2	7.4	33	41%	.309
2018	WNS	A+	22	5	4	0	12	12	77^2	75	5	2.0	6.7	58	56%	.294
2018	BIR	AA	22	3	5	0	13	13	78^1	79	5	1.6	5.4	47	52%	.301
2019	WSX	RK	23	0	0	0	4	4	12	17	2	0.8	9.8	13	54%	.455
2019	BIR	AA	23	3	8	0	15	15	78^1	74	10	1.7	7.9	69	55%	.282
2020	*CHA*	*MLB*	*24*	*2*	*1*	*0*	*14*	*3*	*26*	*25*	*5*	*3.3*	*6.6*	*19*	*49%*	*.271*

Comparables: Jayson Aquino, Jarlin García, Josh Rogers

Flores is a bespectacled baseball nerd who got lost somewhere on the path of becoming an amiable presence on Baseball Twitter and transformed into a full-on baseball player. (To wit, he hoards '80s ballcaps and '90s Starter jackets, and wanders the grounds of Negro League stadiums in his spare time.) True to the genre, the lanky Californian's knowledge of baseball history and pitchability outpace the raw power of his low-90s heater and three-pitch arsenal. Were his share of oblique pulls not as impressive as his memorabilia collection, he would have gotten his shot by now to explore his back-end starter/swingman potential in the majors.

YEAR	TEAM	LVL	AGE	WHIP	ERA	DRA	WARP	MPH	FB%	WHF	CSP
2017	KAN	A	21	1.10	3.00	4.16	1.0				
2017	WNS	A+	21	1.54	4.24	5.44	-0.1				
2018	WNS	A+	22	1.18	2.55	4.43	0.8				
2018	BIR	AA	22	1.19	2.76	4.80	0.5				
2019	WSX	RK	23	1.50	3.75	5.77	0.0				
2019	BIR	AA	23	1.14	3.33	4.40	0.5				
2020	*CHA*	*MLB*	*24*	*1.35*	*4.46*	*4.67*	*0.2*				

Ian Hamilton   RHP

Born: 06/16/95   Age: 25   Bats: R   Throws: R
Height: 6'0"   Weight: 200   Origin: Round 11, 2016 Draft (#326 overall)

YEAR	TEAM	LVL	AGE	W	L	SV	G	GS	IP	H	HR	BB/9	K/9	K	GB%	BABIP
2017	WNS	A+	22	3	3	6	30	0	52^2	33	1	1.4	8.9	52	46%	.241
2017	BIR	AA	22	1	3	1	14	0	19	26	0	3.8	10.4	22	52%	.419
2018	BIR	AA	23	2	1	12	21	0	25^1	20	0	4.3	12.1	34	47%	.323
2018	CHR	AAA	23	1	1	10	22	0	26^1	18	2	1.4	9.6	28	49%	.254
2018	CHA	MLB	23	1	2	0	10	0	8	6	2	2.2	5.6	5	48%	.174
2019	CHR	AAA	24	0	2	3	16	0	16^1	28	4	1.7	11.0	20	53%	.471
2020	CHA	MLB	25	1	1	0	16	0	17	18	3	3.6	8.0	15	46%	.294

Comparables: Chase Whitley, Alejandro Chacin, Jimmy Herget

Hard-throwing reliever Ian, as prominent Hamiltons are seemingly wont to do, took a life-altering shot to the face this past year. He wasn't dueling with a rival or anything like that; instead, he was chilling in the Charlotte dugout when a wayward baseball made a lopsided trade with his face, taking with it several teeth in exchange for a handful of facial fractures that he was allowed to keep for months afterward. And whereas Alexander's shot to the face cut short a government career that at least had more confidently-written documents left in it, the blow to Ian's face could be construed as an act of mercy for a season that had already turned into a nightmare by mid-May. A scary car crash effectively canceled his spring training, a stiff shoulder briefly sapped his velocity, the juiced ball thrashed his hopes of a palatable Triple-A ERA, and that foul ball ended his season. Christmas still proceeded as scheduled.

YEAR	TEAM	LVL	AGE	WHIP	ERA	DRA	WARP	MPH	FB%	WHF	CSP
2017	WNS	A+	22	0.78	1.71	2.40	1.5				
2017	BIR	AA	22	1.79	5.21	6.63	-0.4				
2018	BIR	AA	23	1.26	1.78	3.34	0.5				
2018	CHR	AAA	23	0.84	1.71	2.54	0.8				
2018	CHA	MLB	23	1.00	4.50	3.37	0.1	98.4	70.1	12	46.3
2019	CHR	AAA	24	1.90	9.92	6.53	0.0				
2020	CHA	MLB	25	1.44	5.14	5.16	0.0	98.1	71.8	12.3	47.4

Michael Kopech   RHP

Born: 04/30/96   Age: 24   Bats: R   Throws: R
Height: 6'3"   Weight: 205   Origin: Round 1, 2014 Draft (#33 overall)

YEAR	TEAM	LVL	AGE	W	L	SV	G	GS	IP	H	HR	BB/9	K/9	K	GB%	BABIP
2017	BIR	AA	21	8	7	0	22	22	119^1	77	6	4.5	11.7	155	42%	.272
2017	CHR	AAA	21	1	1	0	3	3	15	15	0	3.0	10.2	17	35%	.375
2018	CHR	AAA	22	7	7	0	24	24	126^1	101	9	4.3	12.1	170	40%	.316
2018	CHA	MLB	22	1	1	0	4	4	14^1	20	4	1.3	9.4	15	28%	.381
2020	CHA	MLB	24	5	5	0	38	11	83	89	18	4.2	7.8	71	36%	.294

Comparables: Tyler Glasnow, Eric Hurley, Logan Allen

A surprise torn UCL (there was no "blow out" moment, just a dispiriting MRI) transformed 2019 from a first full season in the majors for Kopech into a poncho-clad vision quest full of hikes through the desert and self-reflection while he rehabbed in Arizona. For a top pitching prospect who claims his midseason struggles in 2018 were the product of anxiety and even used the term "yips" to describe his Triple-A struggles, a step back from the endless chug of baseball might not be what Kopech ordered, but he wouldn't send it back to the kitchen, either. From more of a purely physical perspective, Kopech was back to throwing his typical upper-90s fastball in instructs by October, albeit with appropriately rusty command, and will be another long, lanky body in spring camp with a curious pink scar running along his underarm by the time February rolls around. He'll just be the strongest one.

YEAR	TEAM	LVL	AGE	WHIP	ERA	DRA	WARP	MPH	FB%	WHF	CSP
2017	BIR	AA	21	1.15	2.87	3.15	2.9				
2017	CHR	AAA	21	1.33	3.00	4.18	0.3				
2018	CHR	AAA	22	1.27	3.70	3.75	2.6				
2018	CHA	MLB	22	1.53	5.02	6.84	-0.3	97.7	62.5	10.9	50.9
2020	CHA	MLB	24	1.54	5.99	5.73	-0.2	97.5	64.4	11.3	52.5

Chicago White Sox 2020

Jimmy Lambert RHP

Born: 11/18/94 Age: 25 Bats: R Throws: R
Height: 6'2" Weight: 190 Origin: Round 5, 2016 Draft (#146 overall)

YEAR	TEAM	LVL	AGE	W	L	SV	G	GS	IP	H	HR	BB/9	K/9	K	GB%	BABIP
2017	KAN	A	22	7	2	0	12	12	74	77	1	1.3	5.2	43	57%	.315
2017	WNS	A+	22	5	4	0	14	14	76	86	10	3.4	7.0	59	50%	.326
2018	WNS	A+	23	5	7	0	13	13	70²	57	5	2.7	10.2	80	46%	.292
2018	BIR	AA	23	3	1	0	5	5	25	20	2	2.2	10.8	30	40%	.286
2019	BIR	AA	24	3	4	0	11	11	59¹	62	11	4.1	10.6	70	38%	.338
2020	CHA	MLB	25	2	2	0	33	0	35	35	6	3.4	8.8	34	38%	.299

Comparables: Dylan Covey, Brandon Woodruff, Travis Lakins

After a year of waning effectiveness as an uninspiring and ignored sinker-slider type, Lambert transformed into a different pitcher thanks to Trackman-inspired tweaks. A shift to a high-fastball, 12-to-6-curveball diet led to swing-and-miss numbers befitting someone with real rotation potential. Alas, not all went well for Lambert. When he went down for Tommy John surgery in June, general manager Rick Hahn tabbed the lanky right-hander as someone who would have gotten a major-league look in 2019 had he stayed healthy, which is like raaaaaaaaaaaaiiiiiiiiiiiiinnnnnn on your wedding day. It's a free riiiiiiiiiiiiiide, when you've already paid. It's the good adviiiiiiiiiiiiiice, that you just didn't take, and who would have thought, he's Peter's brotherrrrrrrr.

YEAR	TEAM	LVL	AGE	WHIP	ERA	DRA	WARP	MPH	FB%	WHF	CSP
2017	KAN	A	22	1.19	2.19	4.78	0.4				
2017	WNS	A+	22	1.51	5.45	6.08	-0.7				
2018	WNS	A+	23	1.10	3.95	3.67	1.4				
2018	BIR	AA	23	1.04	2.88	3.07	0.7				
2019	BIR	AA	24	1.50	4.55	5.57	-0.4				
2020	CHA	MLB	25	1.38	4.64	4.81	0.1				

Jonathan Stiever   RHP

Born: 05/12/97 Age: 23 Bats: R Throws: R
Height: 6'2" Weight: 205 Origin: Round 5, 2018 Draft (#138 overall)

YEAR	TEAM	LVL	AGE	W	L	SV	G	GS	IP	H	HR	BB/9	K/9	K	GB%	BABIP
2018	GRF	RK	21	0	1	0	13	13	28	23	3	2.9	12.5	39	48%	.323
2019	KAN	A	22	4	6	0	14	14	74	88	10	1.7	9.4	77	46%	.361
2019	WNS	A+	22	6	4	0	12	12	71	56	7	1.6	9.8	77	41%	.278
2020	CHA	MLB	23	2	2	0	33	0	35	36	6	3.4	8.2	32	41%	.297

Comparables: Trent Thornton, Felix Jorge, Jordan Smith

Stiever has been someone worth throwing into a big book of baseball players for all of 12 professional starts, which is indicative of them being pretty good. Upon getting promoted to High-A, Stiever got told to "let it eat" up in the zone, and to pair his curve and slider off of that plane. It went at least as well for him as it has gone for the seemingly 5,000 others who have toyed with those levers in the last five years. There's still the whole issue of a changeup that could use more tumble so that lefties are less of an ordeal. But Stiever, originally a Trackman transformation project, now serves as an actual prospect.

YEAR	TEAM	LVL	AGE	WHIP	ERA	DRA	WARP	MPH	FB%	WHF	CSP
2018	GRF	RK	21	1.14	4.18	2.71	1.0				
2019	KAN	A	22	1.38	4.74	6.02	-0.7				
2019	WNS	A+	22	0.97	2.15	3.11	1.7				
2020	CHA	MLB	23	1.40	4.81	4.94	0.1				

LINEOUTS

Hitters

HITTER	POS	TEAM	LVL	AGE	PA	R	2B	3B	HR	RBI	BB	K	SB	CS	AVG/OBP/SLG	DRC+	WARP
Micker Adolfo	OF	BIR	AA	22	95	5	7	0	0	9	14	36	0	3	.205/.337/.295	95	-0.3
	OF	WSX	Rk	22	58	8	5	0	2	3	7	21	0	0	.260/.362/.480	86	-0.3
James Beard	CF	WSX	Rk	18	138	19	4	1	2	12	8	54	9	3	.213/.270/.307	40	-1.1
Nicky Delmonico	LF	CHR	AAA	26	76	13	7	0	3	10	10	12	1	0	.286/.382/.540	131	0.1
	LF	CHA	MLB	26	68	6	2	0	1	6	4	25	0	1	.206/.265/.286	57	-0.1
Alcides Escobar	SS	CHR	AAA	32	405	52	28	0	10	70	32	64	6	2	.286/.343/.444	96	1.5
Yermin Mercedes	C	CHR	AAA	26	220	35	12	0	17	62	24	42	0	0	.310/.386/.647	143	1.6
	C	BIR	AA	26	167	19	7	0	6	18	17	25	2	0	.327/.389/.497	166	2.5
AJ Reed	1B	CHA	MLB	26	49	1	0	0	1	4	4	21	0	0	.136/.204/.205	62	-0.1
	1B	ROU	AAA	26	225	33	11	0	12	35	27	67	0	0	.224/.329/.469	92	0.0
	1B	CHR	AAA	26	42	3	1	0	1	2	2	17	0	0	.179/.238/.282	31	-0.4
Matt Skole	1B	CHR	AAA	29	392	65	15	0	21	56	70	99	0	0	.248/.384/.497	115	0.9
	1B	CHA	MLB	29	80	7	2	0	0	6	7	31	0	0	.208/.275/.236	58	-0.4

Chicago White Sox 2020

Six seasons into his pro career, **Micker Adolfo** is yet to put together a full campaign, most recently because of surgery to clean up his elbow following Tommy John in 2018. The return of a strikeout rate more gargantuan than his raw power adds to the concern that the big outfielder will never live up to his tools. ⓧ Outside of the Royals organization, it's only acceptable to have the profile of "fast but raw in every other baseball aspect" for about a year as a professional. Hopefully **James Beard** enjoys this while it lasts. ⓧ Two Achilles tears have not only kept the former 11th overall pick out of an affiliated game for two seasons, but also made us all too sad to sink our teeth into these juicy burger puns. It's hard to keep the sizzle for **Jake Burger** sticking at third going after such an absence, and even though the raw hitting talent was supposed to be enough to play at first, that's a tall order at this point…a tall order of burgers. His name is Burger. ⓧ There is no official point at which an organization exits a rebuild and enters a contention cycle, but "stops giving playing time to **Nicky Delmonico** seems like a fairly good benchmark. ⓧ It turns out that signing on to be minor-league depth for a rebuilding team that has the AL batting champion at your position locked in through 2024 is *not* a viable route to big-league playing time. Lesson learned for **Alcides Escobar**, who hit okay in Triple-A, saw that it was not going to lead him to a call-up, demanded his release in August, and wasn't heard from again. ⓧ No one is quite sure what defensive position he's capable of manning at the major-league level, or why his massive hand load and ultra-aggressive approach at the plate have not been exploited, or how much upside to assume from a very thickly-built 27-year-old…but dang, *look* at **Yermin Mercedes**' minor league numbers. ⓧ In 2015, we wrote that "Scouting is strange business," as it pertained to **AJ Reed** falling out of the first round despite being a highly productive collegiate. In 2018, we expected that someone would give "this hulk the chance to prove he's either the second coming of Russell Branyan or the second coming of Matt LaPorta." In 2021, we'll concede the scouts were right to have concerns. ⓧ Maybe light-hitting, slick-fielding middle infielders aren't the sexiest profile to be the jewel of your international class. But the Cuban-born **Yolbert Sanchez** got a $2.5 million bonus because he's supposed to be ready to field well (and not hit) in the majors relatively soon. ⓧ Five years in, **Matt Skole** has gotten pretty good—not great—at this whole veteran Triple-A masher lifestyle. This past August, the White Sox took Skole out of his natural habitat. Hijinks ensued, extra-base hits did not.

Pitchers

PITCHER	TEAM	LVL	AGE	W	L	SV	G	GS	IP	H	HR	BB/9	K/9	K	GB%	WHIP	ERA	DRA	WARP
Zack Burdi	BIR	AA	24	0	3	3	17	0	19^2	24	5	5.9	11.0	24	30%	1.88	6.41	6.59	-0.5
Ryan Burr	CHA	MLB	25	1	1	0	16	1	19^2	17	3	3.7	9.2	20	47%	1.27	4.58	4.82	0.1
Ross Detwiler	CHR	AAA	33	1	2	0	8	8	43	44	11	2.3	7.3	35	52%	1.28	3.98	3.71	1.2
	CHA	MLB	33	3	5	0	18	12	69^2	86	20	3.5	5.9	46	52%	1.62	6.59	8.06	-1.8
Matt Foster	BIR	AA	24	0	0	1	6	0	9^2	3	0	1.9	11.2	12	32%	0.52	0.00	2.26	0.3
	CHR	AAA	24	4	1	4	37	0	55	46	9	3.1	10.1	62	37%	1.18	3.76	2.93	1.8
Caleb Frare	CHR	AAA	25	2	1	1	21	0	22^1	22	5	7.7	13.7	34	42%	1.84	7.66	5.04	0.3
	CHA	MLB	25	0	0	0	5	0	2^2	2	1	13.5	10.1	3	29%	2.25	10.12	4.33	0.0
Alec Hansen	WNS	A+	24	1	0	0	9	0	12^2	1	0	5.0	14.9	21	63%	0.63	2.13	1.95	0.4
	BIR	AA	24	1	2	1	30	1	39^2	43	5	8.4	10.2	45	38%	2.02	5.45	7.21	-1.3
Codi Heuer	WNS	A+	22	4	1	2	20	0	38^1	34	0	1.9	10.1	43	63%	1.10	2.82	3.59	0.5
	BIR	AA	22	2	3	9	22	0	29^1	25	0	2.1	6.8	22	66%	1.09	1.84	3.78	0.3
Tyler Johnson	WNS	A+	23	0	1	0	7	0	10	6	1	3.6	13.5	15	73%	1.00	1.80	2.85	0.2
	BIR	AA	23	2	0	0	12	0	18^1	10	3	2.9	11.3	23	36%	0.87	3.44	2.85	0.4
Kodi Medeiros	BIR	AA	23	4	8	0	28	9	83	80	11	5.5	8.1	75	37%	1.58	5.10	6.12	-1.4
Juan Minaya	CHR	AAA	28	4	3	6	24	0	34	32	4	4.0	10.9	41	49%	1.38	3.71	3.47	0.9
	CHA	MLB	28	0	0	0	22	0	27^2	31	4	3.9	8.8	27	29%	1.55	3.90	6.12	-0.2
Konnor Pilkington	KAN	A	21	1	0	0	6	6	33^1	15	2	3.0	11.3	42	35%	0.78	1.62	2.18	1.2
	WNS	A+	21	4	9	0	19	19	95^2	99	7	3.7	9.0	96	38%	1.44	4.99	5.69	-0.8
Hector Santiago	CHR	AAA	31	1	4	0	7	7	37	45	9	2.2	8.0	33	37%	1.46	5.84	5.47	0.4
	SYR	AAA	31	3	1	0	8	7	43	32	5	4.8	8.0	38	42%	1.28	3.35	5.07	0.7
	CHA	MLB	31	0	1	0	11	2	25^2	32	7	6.0	11.9	34	35%	1.91	6.66	7.43	-0.5
	NYN	MLB	31	1	0	0	8	0	8	10	1	5.6	6.8	6	22%	1.88	6.75	8.61	-0.3
Thyago Vieira	CHR	AAA	25	6	4	8	39	0	47^1	53	7	4.2	9.7	51	52%	1.58	5.70	4.97	0.6
	CHA	MLB	25	1	0	0	6	0	7	11	0	6.4	10.3	8	38%	2.29	9.00	6.86	-0.1

Some control problems aside, **Zack Burdi** (the younger brother of Nick) was pushing for a big-league call-up barely a year after being drafted when his elbow blew out in July 2017. Between an extended Tommy John rehab, a lat strain, and now knee surgery, that fire-breathing form has yet to be seen since. ⓧ White Sox relievers Ian Hamilton and **Ryan Burr** played up their historic namesakes for laughs in a spring training skit. But in keeping with the theme, Hamilton's spring training was derailed by a car crash and a foul ball to the face, and Burr keeps photoshopping googly eyes over Instagram posts of his Tommy John scar. Duels are bad, kids. ⓧ Unless you were so good at something in high school that you asked for $2 million to skip college and turn professional, you cannot relate to **Andrew Dalquist**, whose senior-year velocity jump matched up with the excitement his easy delivery inspired in scouts. As a lauded high-school pitching prospect, Dalquist probably cannot relate to his peers in a college-heavy Sox system, but maybe he can pass them up. ⓧ It seems like a bygone era when **Ross Detwiler** was drafted sixth overall. Judging by the way hitters treated his sinker in 2019—.338 batting average, .636 slugging percentage, and 6.9 percent whiff rate—it was. ⓫ Safe, reliable strike-throwing from a tall, sturdy frame with consistent success into the upper minors are soothing qualities for a pitching prospect profile. A season and a half of inaction due to elbow troubles and eventual Tommy John surgery are less so, but such is life for **Dane Dunning**, who will likely continue rehabbing until midway through 2020. ⓫ Alabama has been good to right-handed reliever **Matt Foster** from his illustrious high school career at Valley to his impressive junior season in Tuscaloosa to his scoreless streak to start the 2019 season in Birmingham, and he now finds himself knocking on the door to the White Sox bullpen. ⓫ **Caleb Frare** got himself to the majors by ceasing to worry about control and just throwing the ball as hard as he could. But despite winning an Opening Day roster spot, his velocity backing up only made everyone worry about his flighty control even more. The three-batter minimum won't be good news for his career even if some mid-90s juice returns. ⓫ **Alec Hansen** had an outstanding pro debut. He's struggled since, resulting in a shift to the 'pen. It didn't help, given he walked 103 batters in 103 innings. We're optimistic about his prospects. It's three truths and a lie, folks —here's a hint: they're in order. ⓫ With the White Sox having spent only a half-season wasting time on the illusion that **Codi Heuer's** control issues would get worked out as a starter, they will likely will have to wait only that much longer for him to reach the majors. The plus life on his fastball weighs just as heavily on his profile as any concerns about the strikeout dip in Double-A. ⓫ **Tyler Johnson's** crossfiring ways finally caught up with him last season in the form of a lat strain that swallowed half of his year. When he played, there were no signs yet that platoon issues will limit him to middle relief. ⓫ Minor-league pitcher wins and losses are the only thing dumber than the major-league version, but it sure is something that former first rounder **Kodi Medeiros** managed to drop 10 decisions in a row after being traded to the White Sox. It wasn't like he was secretly pitching well while his team lost before the Sox converted him to relief, just as it's not like that switch led him to throw more strikes. ⓫ To get outrighted and go unclaimed on waivers is a dispiriting career low-point. To battle back to the majors in the same season is a demonstration of determination. To get outrighted and go unclaimed on waivers twice in the same season is the sort of oddity that makes its way into a year-end comment. Here's to you, **Juan Minaya**. ⓫ The burly left-hander's selling points after a decorated career at Mississippi State were polish and deception rather than raw stuff. Therefore **Konnor Pilkington** racking up big strikeout numbers while barely cracking 90 mph, but struggling to stanch big innings in High-A, is more odd than encouraging. ⓫ Given the progression of the printing industry and human society, we have to prepare for the strong possibility that **Héctor Santiago** will be making a small collection of valiant but ineffective spot starts years after the discontinuance of this publication. It will probably be for the White Sox, as he remains the most successful member of their 2006 draft class, despite being taken in the 30th round. ⓫ A 2019 draft light on college pitching finally nudged the White Sox into the prep market. Once there, they swung big to land **Matthew Thompson**, a multi-sport star in Houston (he can sing too) who has all the athleticism and projection you would want in a teenage pitcher, as well as the strike-throwing consistency issues you would expect. ⓧ **Thyago Vieira** hit a legit 102 mph on the radar gun at Triple-A Charlotte in August. His post-save celebrations answer the hypothetical of what the "Ace Ventura" movies would be like if they were remade starring a 230-pound Brazilian man wearing rec specs. Other than that, he's a drag to watch.

White Sox Prospects

The State of the System

The White Sox still have a few close-to-ready high-end prospect cards to play as they transition to AL Central contenders, but past that things thin out more quickly than recent years.

The Top Ten

★ ★ ★ *2020 Top 101 Prospect* **#6** ★ ★ ★

1
Luis Robert   OF   OFP: 70   ETA: 2020
Born: 08/03/97   Age: 22   Bats: R   Throws: R   Height: 6'3"   Weight: 185
Origin: International Free Agent, 2017

The Report: Watching him scuffle through an injury-plagued 2018, there was an air of creeping disappointment unable yet to stifle great hopes and expectations. Watching him swing through hittable pitches and lousy breaking balls, unable to tap into his power, one knew there had to be something there that had made Robert the most talked about international talent in years. Just wait until he's right.

Well, he healed up in 2019 and proved all he had to at the minor league level. A true five-tool player with a whiff of purely hypothetical uncertainty about the hit, La Pantera preyed on pitchers across three levels while playing a beautiful center field and swiping bases by the bundle. An incredible athlete, Robert has excellent speed underway but typically makes the plays simply by gliding. He's similarly quiet and assured at the plate with a smooth swing that produces good bat speed and has some lift to it for easy plus power. He can catch up to the hard stuff and his approach against breaking balls has taken leaps; he is now able to lay off spin when it is out of the zone while reserving the ability to adjust, wait back, and drive to all fields when he finds one to his liking.

If there is one ephemeral worry surrounding Robert it is that old demons could crop up when he is faced with top shelf breaking stuff, and that this could dampen his hit tool a bit. Still, he's shown the aptitude to make adjustments when necessary and is strong enough everywhere else that the profile can overcome a slight lag in his fifth tool. At this time, it is a very select group of prospects we'd take over this cat.

Variance: Low. He's big-league ready and probably has been since midseason. His hit tool carries risk but he will contribute even if he ends up hitting for a low average.

Ben Carsley's Fantasy Take: That pesky Jo Adell guy keeps Robert from earning the distinction of the top outfield prospect in dynasty, but our protagonist ranks only one spot behind. Aside from some boo boos on his resume, Robert has everything you could want in a prospect: A high upside, a high floor and a fantasy-friendly ETA (even more so post-contract extension). If it all clicks, we're looking at a bonafide OF1 capable of contributing substantially across all five categories. But even if Robert's hit tool fails to fully actualize, he's got enough power and speed to serve as a fine OF3. Congrats if you bought in on the hype way back when; it looks justified.

─────── ★ ★ ★ *2020 Top 101 Prospect* **#13** ★ ★ ★ ───────

2

Nick Madrigal 2B OFP: 70 ETA: 2020
Born: 03/05/97 Age: 23 Bats: R Throws: R Height: 5'7" Weight: 165
Origin: Round 1, 2018 Draft (#4 overall)

The Report: Madrigal has extreme, extreme bat-to-ball ability, essentially off the charts; he struck out a grand total of 16 times across 532 plate appearances this season. He doesn't do that by constantly hacking away at bad pitches either, like Willians Astudillo has, and Astudillo is the only other current affiliated player who has demonstrated this level of contact ability. Madrigal's walk and swing rates are more or less normal. He just doesn't miss when he swings, and it doesn't lead to off-balance or poor contact.

What Madrigal doesn't do yet is hit the ball consistently hard. He has below-average raw, and he's yet to attempt the trade-off to even get to that in games. His offensive game is to shoot the ball between the defense, not over it, and that's unusual for today's game of optimized launch angles and focus on exit velocity. He will provide secondary value with his defense (he's quite good at second base, and the White Sox have made prior noise about trying him at short) and speed (plus-plus, and he uses it well on the basepaths). But we can't project him for much more than 40 game power, and he's not even there yet.

So what should you make of all this? We see an outlier profile with a good shot for a batting average that is consistently starting with 3 and carries the rest of the profile. If you're a little less sanguine about his ability to hit 'em where they ain't, that's going to be closer to a David Eckstein or late-career Marco Scutaro offensive profile, but that isn't so bad either.

Variance: Low, although the fair over/under on batting crowns is probably more like 0.5 on his median outcome. He's one of the highest floor prospects in the game, an unusually safe bet to be at least a decent regular because of his already existent contact/defense/speed.

Ben Carsley's Fantasy Take: Only 21 batters stole 20 or more bases last season, and only 10 of those batters had infield eligibility. Only 19 (qualified) batters hit above .300 last season, and only 11 of them had infield eligibility. Madrigal lacks pop, it's true, but he's a genuine threat to hit .300 with 25-plus steals on a regular basis, and he could score a ton of runs, too. There's some slight Fancy Dog Jose Peraza risk in the profile, but there's a better chance that Madrigal is the spiritual successor to some of those early day Elvis Andrus stat lines. He's an easy top-20 dynasty prospect.

★ ★ ★ *2020 Top 101 Prospect* **#20** ★ ★ ★

3 **Michael Kopech   RHP**   OFP: 70   ETA: 2018
Born: 04/30/96   Age: 24   Bats: R   Throws: R   Height: 6'3"   Weight: 205
Origin: Round 1, 2014 Draft (#33 overall)

The Report: As expected, Kopech missed the entire year recovering from Tommy John surgery. Steve Givarz saw him rehabbing in instructs in the fall, and he was sitting 97-98 and touched 101. So, basically, he looked like Michael Kopech. He's expected to have a relatively normal spring and should be a rotation factor again during the first half.

When healthy, Kopech sits in the mid-to-high-90s with his fastball and regularly touches triple-digits; he hit 105 mph on a Boston charting gun in 2016, and he's said his goal is to hit 107. His best offspeed pitch is a nasty, wipeout slider in the low-to-mid-80s. That pitch has sharp, two-plane break, and it's a true swing-and-miss pitch and a potential plus-plus offering. He also supplements with a changeup that was improving to more of a true third pitch from a prior show-me level, and flashes a nice slower curve from time to time.

Kopech has battled significant bouts of wildness in the past, and at times has dialed his stuff a bit back to get better command and control. Steve noted in his instructs look that Kopech's command wasn't all the way back yet, and that's going to be a key storyline to follow with him early in the season.

Variance: Medium. Kopech was in the majors when he got hurt and is generally pretty fully-formed. The wildness and Tommy John do add a dash of relief risk, although he'd be a monster there.

Ben Carsley's Fantasy Take: This system is fun. I have long served as the BP Fantasy Team's resident Kopech apologist, and I'm not jumping off the bandwagon now. Few if any arms in the minors can match Kopech's pure strikeout potential, and he should see significant MLB time in 2020. The catch of course is that Kopech is likely to take in WHIP what he gives in Ks, and there's still enough command/control risk that he could end up a reliever. My personal bet is that Kopech reigns it in just enough to serve as a (Tampa Bay Rays) Chris Archer-esque fantasy SP3 who provides you with 200-plus strikeouts. That makes him a top-30ish fantasy prospect in my book, but if you're lower on him you're not crazy.

── ★ ★ ★ *2020 Top 101 Prospect* **#31** ★ ★ ★ ──

4   **Andrew Vaughn   1B**   OFP: 60   ETA: 2021
Born: 04/03/98   Age: 22   Bats: R   Throws: R   Height: 6'0"   Weight: 214
Origin: Round 1, 2019 Draft (#3 overall)

The Report: Vaughn isn't the most viscerally thrilling of top five picks, but he is a pretty safe bet to be a productive if unglamourous big leaguer. He didn't have a particularly strong professional debut, but this is understandable. Asked to jump into full-season ball almost immediately after the conclusion of his college campaign, the 21-year-old was saddled with big expectations and asked to make big adjustments on the fly while presumably dealing with some level of fatigue. His tools at the plate were apparent anyway, led by excellent discipline that doesn't waver when he slumps and allows him to limit swing-and-miss while zeroing in on pitches in particular zones where he does damage. Pair this with his barrel control and you have a plus hit tool with low strikeout rates and a lot of hard contact. The power is also plus, driven by a quick bat and strength that is easily visible in both the upper and lower halves. He's fine at first but won't add a lot of value with his defense.

Variance: Low. Offensive game is well-developed, just needs to prove it at the upper levels.

Ben Carsley's Fantasy Take: Yes, Vaughn is a first base prospect, but he's easily the best one in the minors, and his combination of floor, ETA, and reasonable ceiling make him a very strong fantasy asset. We have Vaughn as the best player available in first-year supplemental drafts—ahead even of Adley Rutschman, because catchers are weird—as well as a top-10 overall fantasy prospect. I know—I was surprised when I saw the rankings, too—but the more you hear about Vaughn's bat, the more you understand it. Don't overthink this one; pursue Vaughn aggressively wherever you can.

5   **Jonathan Stiever   RHP**   OFP: 55   ETA: 2021
Born: 05/12/97   Age: 23   Bats: R   Throws: R   Height: 6'2"   Weight: 205
Origin: Round 5, 2018 Draft (#138 overall)

The Report: A fifth-rounder from a cold-weather state, Stiever began his professional career slowly but caused a lot of antennae to fly up with an excellent three months or so in the Carolina League following a June promotion. The Hoosier dominated High-A hitters with a plus fastball that explodes up in the zone and gets some sink down, sitting a lively 95 and topping out at 97. The curve is a potential plus pitch as well, a powerful offering in the low-to-mid 80s. This pitch is best when he hits a particular sweet spot of velocity and movement; he can get both horizontal and lateral movement on the pitch, with about a 10-4 break and sharp downward action paired with slider-like glove-side cut. He'll also throw a change-of-pace curve in the mid-70s and a decent mid-80s change, and he would do well to make the latter more prominent in his arsenal. He's a joy to watch, outwardly competitive and a great athlete with a sound delivery that portends future strides in fastball command.

Variance: Medium. Has many of the characteristics of a mid-rotation starter or possibly even a No. 2, but at present he is essentially a two-pitch pitcher whose command is a work in progress.

Ben Carsley's Fantasy Take: And now the fun ends. Stiever is a nice filler prospect for those of you in deeper leagues, as he has reasonable upside and pretty much no name value right now. That being said, he's still just somewhere in the giant glut of potential fantasy SP5/6 prospects who need a third pitch, better command, or both. Don't consider biting unless your league rosters around 200 dudes.

6. Dane Dunning   RHP
OFP: 55   ETA: Late 2020
Born: 12/20/94   Age: 25   Bats: R   Throws: R   Height: 6'4"   Weight: 200
Origin: Round 1, 2016 Draft (#29 overall)

The Report: Dunning was one of last spring's Tommy John blowouts after missing time at the end of 2018 with arm problems. He's going to be behind Kopech on his rehab schedule, but he's throwing off a mound already and should be back in game action at some point in 2020, barring setbacks. He was knocking on the door of the majors before going down, so if he comes back early and at full strength, he could be up quickly.

Before going down, Dunning had established himself as a four-pitch, back of the 101-quality mid-rotation starting prospect. His fastball is in the low-90s, which is close to average velocity these days, but has heavy sink and run. That movement, along with plus command, cause the pitch to play up from its velocity a bit. Dunning throws two breaking balls: A hard, nearly-cutterish slider that has a shot to get to plus, and a big bendy curveball that should settle in at average or a touch above. He also mixes in a changeup that flashes, but needs improvement.

Variance: Medium. Tommy John rehab is a risk factor, and he's going to be returning as 25-year-old with a total of 62 innings in the high-minors, but Dunning is relatively "safe" as mid-rotation prospects go.

Ben Carsley's Fantasy Take: See Stiever, Jon, but factor in that Dunning has some more name value since he's been around longer. If someone (reasonably) cut bait after his Tommy John, feel free to re-add him if you're in a TDGX-sized (200-plus prospects) league. Just don't expect front-end SP production.

7. Luis Alexander Basabe   OF
OFP: 50   ETA: 2020/21
Born: 08/26/96   Age: 23   Bats: B   Throws: R   Height: 6'0"   Weight: 160
Origin: International Free Agent, 2012

The Report: We are still waiting for Basabe to put it all together, and that's beginning to become a problem. To be fair, injuries have plagued his pro career. Last year, a broken hamate in spring training and a quad injury in June limited him to just 75 games. At a certain point—perhaps right around when you turn 23 or so—those patterns of injuries start to become "durability concerns." And yes, hamate injuries tend to sap power, which would explain some of why Basabe only hit three home runs in a half-season in Birmingham despite above-average raw power, but in total he's hit .248/.345/.392 across 130 Double-A games. He'll be 24 next year and projection only takes you so far now.

The thing is, the underlying prospect still looks pretty good. Basabe offers bat speed from both sides of the plate, although an aggressive approach undermines him too often. There's power potential from the left side, although he can get longer to tap into it, while his right-handed swing shoots the gaps more. He continues to see time at all three outfield spots, but should have enough foot speed for center and enough arm for right. The whole package looks more like a good fourth outfielder now—which was the risk with the profile going back to his Red Sox days—but you can still squint and blame the injuries some and see a starter if you'd like. At least for one more year.

Variance: High. Basabe may just not hit enough for anything more than an extra bench outfielder role. The injuries have sapped the tools a bit at this point as well. But then he will have games where he looks like a sure shot outfield starter, so you keep squinting to see it during the IL stints and bad weeks.

Ben Carsley's Fantasy Take: I'm about ready to hop off the Basabe bandwagon, which probably means he's about to turn into Mike Trout. The lack of power doesn't concern me given his hamate injury. I'm more worried about Basabe's hit tool, and in total the upside here just isn't high enough to justify the risk. He's close enough that he's arguably still worth rostering if you keep 200-250 prospects, but I'd also be fine cutting bait. It's hard to see him as more than a fourth or fifth outfielder at this point.

8. Zack Collins C   OFP: 45   ETA: 2019
Born: 02/06/95 Age: 25 Bats: L Throws: R Height: 6'3" Weight: 220
Origin: Round 1, 2016 Draft (#10 overall)

The Report: As his 2019 Annual comment suggests, Collins came around about a decade too late to be a top catching prospect. In another era he'd be ranked with the Jeff Clements and J.P. Arenecibias of the prospect world. Power hitters with plus arms, not much else to catching, right? Collins' power is real, and although the rabbit ball certainly helped him, he's always had plus raw power and enough of an idea what he could pull 400 feet to get to it in games. There's stiffness and bat wrap as well though, meaning strikeouts come in bunches, but if he could stick behind the plate and hit .230 or .240 or so, he'd be a viable starter given how low the bar for catcher offense is.

The bar for catcher defense however, has changed a lot since the mid-2000s. Even coming out of college, the grade on Collins glove was—to put it kindly—"needs improvement." He's a big lad, and a stiff receiver at best. His CSAA rate stat in the majors—in an admittedly small sample—was bottom 10 among the 113 catchers in baseball last year. His Triple-A numbers were not much better. He spent more time at first base and DH in the majors than he did behind the plate, and he might be best suited as a Sunday backup who you can start elsewhere during the week.

Variance: Low. Collins' bat is as ready for the majors as it will ever be, although his first go-round featured a fair bit of flailing at stuff on the outer half. He also might be the one player in baseball who would be helped the most by an automated strike zone, although that may come too late to help him stick behind the plate.

Ben Carsley's Fantasy Take: I told you to stay away from catching prospects. Stay away from catching prospects.

9 Gavin Sheets   1B   OFP: 50   ETA: 2020/21
Born: 04/23/96   Age: 24   Bats: L   Throws: L   Height: 6'4"   Weight: 230
Origin: Round 2, 2017 Draft (#49 overall)

The Report: Sheets has maintained a slow but steady climb up the organizational ladder since he was a second-round pick in 2017. He finally showed positionally appropriate game pop in Double-A, which is a positive sign. He has the strength and physicality for 20 home runs in the majors despite keeping everything relatively quiet and compact through the zone for a hitter of his size. Sheets does tend to get pull-happy and doesn't lift the ball as consistently as you'd like to feel confident in a plus power projection, and it's more likely to play merely above-average. The hit tool is average-ish due to the aforementioned propensity to try and pull everything to right field, and some issues with spin generally. There isn't anything particularly positive or negative to say about his first base defense. He moves well for a dude with a XXL frame, and shows good hands in the field and on scoops.

Variance: Medium. There's not so much game power in here that he can survive seeing the hit tool diminished against better arms, and he was merely fine, not spectacular against Double-A ones.

Ben Carsley's Fantasy Take: I will never be free of this pain.

10 Lenyn Sosa   SS   OFP: 50   ETA: 2022
Born: 01/25/00   Age: 20   Bats: R   Throws: R   Height: 6'0"   Weight: 180
Origin: International Free Agent, 2016

The Report: Sosa has generated some hype in White Sox prospect fan circles over the last year or so, and the reasons for this are understandable enough. He has a name that rolls off the tongue and is easily memorable, and he has the look of a type of high-upside youth that the Sox haven't quite filled lists with in recent years. It might surprise some to hear it, but the main question in the profile is probably how high this upside actually is. The 20-year-old isn't really physically projectible, standing at about 6-foot and listed at a mostly filled-out 180 lbs. His game doesn't really have glaring weaknesses. He's very sound at short with the range, hands, action and arm to cover the rest of the diamond. He's a pretty good contact hitter who can adjust to different pitch types, fast and breaking. The bat speed is fine and he has some pop. I wouldn't be concerned with the pedestrian production considering age and level but I'd like to see one or two of these skills develop into a carrying tool, and this is far from a guarantee.

Variance: High. There is a lot that needs to happen here but he's still very young.

Ben Carsley's Fantasy Take: Too far away and with too meh of a ceiling (industry term) to be of interest to us. Add him to your watch list if you must.

The Next Ten

11
Andrew Dalquist   RHP
Born: 11/13/00   Age: 19   Bats: R   Throws: R   Height: 6'1"   Weight: 175
Origin: Round 3, 2019 Draft (#81 overall)

12
Matthew Thompson   RHP
Born: 08/11/00   Age: 19   Bats: R   Throws: R   Height: 6'3"   Weight: 195
Origin: Round 2, 2019 Draft (#45 overall)

Take your pick of projectable prep arms. The White Sox took them a round apart and gave both around $2 million to sign. We prefer Dalquist—the third-round pick—a smidge more at present due to his combination of present stuff and future projection. He already shows average fastball velocity, and will flash good two-seam run on the pitch. It's not hard to see a 55 or better pitch as he fills out and adds strength. The curveball is the best present secondary. Dalquist has advanced feel for the mid-70s breaker although he can snap it off at times. He also shows a slider and changeup. The delivery is uptempo with a bit of late effort, but it shouldn't be hard to smooth out if he stays a starter.

Thompson is a tall, high-waisted, athletic Texas prep arm right out of central casting. He's at times shown a bit more velocity than Dalquist, and he's got big arm speed, but his radar readings have been more inconsistent as an amateur. He offers the same four-pitch mix, but neither breaker is as advanced as Dalquist's curve, although both have the potential to be above-average. There's a bit more torque and head whack in the delivery when he's ramping up on the fastball, so there's a bit more command and reliever risk here.

Both pitchers made brief pro cameos in the complex and are conservatively four years away from the bigs. It's perhaps a bit of a punt to cast them both as potential No. 3 or 4 starters or late inning relievers, as their profiles will no doubt ebb and flow over the balance of the half-decade. Pitches will improve, injuries will happen, sands will pass through the hourglass, but that's where we are for this particular snapshot in time.

13 Luis González   OF
Born: 09/10/95   Age: 24   Bats: L   Throws: L   Height: 6'1"   Weight: 195
Origin: Round 3, 2017 Draft (#87 overall)

González struggled a bit with the jump to Double-A after a minor breakout in 2018. The profile remains broadly the same. Despite a bit of a noisy set-up and double toe tap, González makes a decent amount of contact from the left side with gap power. The swing plane is fairly flat, and can be geared for all-fields contact, so the game power is likely to top out in the low double-digits. He's an average runner, perhaps a tick above, and has experience at all three outfield spots, and often played center last year over both Basabe and Blake Rutherford. He's passable there for now, but there remain a lot of tweener/fourth outfield profile markers here.

14 Jimmy Lambert   LHP
Born: 11/18/94   Age: 25   Bats: R   Throws: R   Height: 6'2"   Weight: 190
Origin: Round 5, 2016 Draft (#146 overall)

Lambert looked to continue his 2018 breakout into 2019, and despite the velocity dipping back into the low-90s, he got off to a strong start in Double-A mixing in his above-average curve and average change. Toward the end of May he started to lose the strike zone and give up some bombs, and then came the dreaded discovery of a UCL tear. Lambert had Tommy John surgery in the summer and will likely miss all of 2020 as well. He will be 26 before he throws another pitch, but the potential four-pitch mix here remains intriguing—if backend starterish—assuming a normal rehab.

15 Yolbert Sanchez   SS
Born: 03/03/97   Age: 23   Bats: R   Throws: R   Height: 5'11"   Weight: 176
Origin: International Free Agent, 2019

Signed out of Cuba last July for $2.5 million, Sanchez is already 22 and has three seasons under his belt in Serie Nacional. Far from a tools monster, Sanchez is a polished contact hitter with a potential plus shortstop glove. There's almost no power in the profile, so how well the bat translates to professional pitching in the minors will dictate whether he's more of a defensive specialist bench piece or a potential everyday player at the 6. Sanchez only played in the DSL last summer—likely for tax purposes—but 2020 should clear up some things with regards to his future projection.

16 Micker Adolfo OF
Born: 09/11/96 Age: 23 Bats: R Throws: R Height: 6'4" Weight: 255
Origin: International Free Agent, 2013

As a remix of all the pitchers in this organization coming off Tommy John surgery, here's a hitter coming off the surgery. Elbow damage has marred Adolfo's last two seasons. He suffered a partial UCL tear early in 2018 spring training, which limited him to DH duties until he underwent surgery late that summer. He was DHing again in Double-A this April when he went down with complications in his elbow that kept him out until complex action in August. He did show up in the Arizona Fall League and finally played some outfield, which is a good sign. Adolfo has absolutely massive raw power and has a crazy athletic frame, so there remains a lot to dream on here. But he's struggled to get to all of his raw into games because of persistent swing-and-miss problems, and missing as much developmental time as he has missed presents a big hurdle. At the very least, he might be an awful lot of fun in Triple-A if the rocket ball remains.

17 Bryce Bush 3B/OF
Born: 12/14/99 Age: 20 Bats: R Throws: R Height: 6'0" Weight: 200
Origin: Round 33, 2018 Draft (#978 overall)

Bush wasn't expected to sign as a 33th-round pick in the 2018 draft, but the White Sox offered him Day 2 money and bought him out of his college commitment to Mississippi State. The results have been mixed so far, although the South Atlantic League was an aggressive assignment for Bush in his first full pro season. The raw power and bat speed are still obvious, but he's moved off third base—not unexpectedly—to right field. The tools profile is a better fit there, but he struggled with full-season spin, and a bout of bronchitis kept him off the field most of the summer. There was always going to be a long developmental window with Bush, but the overall forecast of his bat remains a bit cloudier than you'd like after 2019.

18 Bernardo Flores LHP
Born: 08/23/95 Age: 24 Bats: L Throws: L Height: 6'2" Weight: 190
Origin: Round 7, 2016 Draft (#206 overall)

Either side of a mid-season oblique injury, Flores kept on puttering through the minors mixing his pitches and keeping baseballs off the fat part of the bat. A solidly built lefty with an uptempo delivery with a bit of funk, he pounds both sides of the plate with a low-90s fastball that he uses to set up his array of secondaries. The changeup is his best offspeed pitch, with 10+ mph of velocity separation and arm speed that sells it as the fastball. He can steal a strike with his humpy, low-70s curve and a short, cutterish slider offers a different breaking ball look to lefties. Nothing here grades out all that better than average, and Flores has been consistently old for his levels, but he's a durable, useful utility arm who could fit in a bunch of different roles on a modern major-league staff most likely as a bulk innings guy or swingman.

19 Konnor Pilkington LHP
Born: 09/12/97   Age: 22   Bats: L   Throws: L   Height: 6'3"   Weight: 225
Origin: Round 3, 2018 Draft (#81 overall)

A third-rounder in 2018 out of Mississippi State, Pilkington was known early in his collegiate career for a mid-90s heater that he could pair with decent secondaries. The stuff has backed up since then, and his reputation as a prospect has ebbed significantly throughout his pro career. The 22-year-old dominated Low-A Kannapolis early this season but struggled after a promotion to High-A Winston-Salem. Currently sitting around 88-91 and flashing occasional run and sink, the fastball gets hit when it is not located precisely and will require a command bump if it is to be effective against hitters at the higher levels. The curve is interesting, ranging from the mid-70s to the mid-80s and showing varying types of break. The pitch comes in around 10-4 or 11-5 on the lower end and is almost a distinct offering in the upper velo bands, featuring short cutter-like movement that could turn it into a weapon against opposite-hand hitters. The change is fine and has a bit of split-action, but nothing that will propel his arsenal to another level. With command refinements he might be able to make it as a back-end starter, but the lack of any premium ingredients makes Pilkington a risky proposition.

20 Blake Rutherford OF
Born: 05/02/97   Age: 23   Bats: L   Throws: R   Height: 6'2"   Weight: 210
Origin: Round 1, 2016 Draft (#18 overall)

On 2016 draft day, it seemed likely Rutherford and Mickey Moniak would be linked together as prep outfield prospects much the way Clint Frazier and Austin Meadows were. I guess it's worked out that way…sort of, as both have been relatively disappointing as pros. Rutherford and Moniak were considered two of the safest prep bats in recent memory. Rutherford was older as a prep pick and more likely to move to a corner, perhaps two reasons—along with bonus demands—that he fell out of the top half of the first round, but we always thought he'd hit. More swing-and-miss creeped into his game in Double-A and Rutherford continues to struggle against same-side pitching. The swing lacks loft and at this point it's hard to predict Rutherford growing into more power without a fairly significant swing change. Like Moniak, he looks more like a bench outfielder than a starter, but he lacks his draft counterparts center field glove, making it a tougher profile in the majors.

Personal Cheeseball

Alec Hansen   RHP
Born: 10/10/94   Age: 25   Bats: R   Throws: R   Height: 6'7"   Weight: 235
Origin: Round 2, 2016 Draft (#49 overall)

Well, this hasn't gone so well recently. Just two offseasons ago, Hansen was a top 50 global prospect coming off an utterly dominant season as a starter. He was still a little riskier than most advanced college arms who tore through A-ball with premium stuff because of a history of wildness, but it looked like just that: history. Then he came into spring in 2018 and suffered a forearm injury, and he's largely been unable to throw strikes since. He converted to relief in 2019, and mixed flashes of dominance there with the same control problems. He's a giant, and we comped Dellin Betances here last year as another tall mid-90s fastball/power breaking ball prospect who couldn't throw strikes in the high-minors but eventually got it together to become an elite reliever. Every year Hansen doesn't pull it together, that sort of outcome gets a little further away, but he's only 25 and the stuff is still there somewhere…

Low Minors Sleeper

James Beard   OF
Born: 09/24/00   Age: 19   Bats: R   Throws: R   Height: 5'10"   Weight: 170
Origin: Round 4, 2019 Draft (#110 overall)

Potentially the fastest player in the 2020 draft class, the White Sox fourth-round pick is an 80-grade runner who will need significant development time on the rest of the profile. Because of the speed, you'll likely hear some Billy Hamilton comps, but he reminds me a bit more of a stronger Anfrenee Seymour at present. Whether that added physicality allows him to generate more game power than Hamilton or Seymour have been able to will be key to his professional development. The hit tool is extremely raw at present as well. Despite his speed he still needs some work on the grass as well, but players with that kind of straight line speed almost always end up of above-average in center field.

Top Talents 25 and Under (as of 4/1/2020)

1. Yoan Moncada
2. Lucas Giolito
3. Eloy Jimenez
4. Luis Robert
5. Nick Madrigal
6. Michael Kopech
7. Dylan Cease
8. Andrew Vaughn
9. Jonathan Stiever
10. Dane Dunning

Robert rightfully ranks highly on the Top 101, so the fact that three names appear ahead of his speaks to the young talent the White Sox have graduated to the major-league level in recent years.

It's kind of hard to fathom, but amid Tim Anderson's bat flips and batting title, and Lucas Giolito's bounce-back All-Star season, Moncada's 2019 performance seemed to fly under-the-radar. The former top prospect was the White Sox best player, putting up a 123 DRC+ and 5.1 WARP season despite missing 30 games. He hit 25 home runs, stole 10 bags, and proved more than competent defensively after a move back to third base. He turned into the type of talent we'd long anticipated.

Giolito's turnaround from one of the worst pitchers in baseball to legitimate ace was close to unprecedented. The right-hander abandoned his sinker entirely and upped his fastball usage while turning his changeup into a devastating weapon. He doubled his strikeout rate (16 percent to 32 percent) and chopped three percentage points off his walk rate. About the only thing he didn't accomplish was crossing the 200-inning mark, as the White Sox played it safe with him down the stretch after a minor injury and shut him down for the last month.

Jimenez's season mirrored Moncada's 2018 in a way, as the slugger we ranked as the fourth-best prospect in baseball before last year showed plenty of potential while enduring injuries and growing pains in an uneven rookie year. The power played as expected—his HR/FB was the eighth-highest mark in the majors—but he also whiffed a ton and hardly walked (he finished the year with

31 home runs and 30 walks) while his defense in left field was … adventurous, to put it kindly. Jimenez still has all the makings of the middle-of-the-order masher many envisioned, he just hasn't put it all together quite yet.

The only other non-prospect-eligible player on the list is Cease, who missed a lot of bats and a lot of the plate in a 14-start rookie year following a midseason call-up. He has elite stuff, but didn't always know where it was going. He slots in behind Kopech based solely on ceiling despite Kopech's uncertainty following Tommy John surgery.

Part 3: Featured Articles

The Baseball Is Juiced (Again)

Robert Arthur

This article originally appeared at Baseball Prospectus on April 5, 2019.

It started when the normally reliable Chris Sale got lit up for three homers by the Mariners in the Red Sox's season opener. It was part of a record number of taters that flew on Opening Day, as starters from Sale to Zack Greinke were taken deep by the handful. Then Christian Yelich hit a home run in each of his first four games, tying yet another MLB record, this one for consecutive games with a dinger to start a season.

It didn't take long for fans and players to begin whispering and tweeting about the baseballs being juiced again. It's early yet for us to come to any definitive conclusion about the 2019 season, but preliminary data shows that the baseball has returned to its aerodynamic peak. Whether that means this season will smash home run records like 2017 did remains to be seen.

Before home run explosion over the last few years, no one worried too much about the baseball's air resistance. While MLB and Rawlings (the company that manufactures the official baseballs) kept track of dozens of metrics to make sure that the ball was consistent from month to month, they didn't measure drag.

But drag is incredibly important in determining how likely a hitter is to knock one out of the park. As baseballs become more aerodynamic, they travel further given a certain initial velocity. A deep fly ball that might have been caught at the warning track can instead go into the first row of the stands. A three percent change in drag coefficient can work to add about five feet to a well-hit fly ball, which can in turn increase home runs league wide by an astounding 10-15 percent.

It's possible to measure the aerodynamics of the baseball using the pitch-tracking radars currently in place in each MLB ballpark. By calculating the loss of speed from when the pitch is released to when it crosses the plate, you can directly measure the drag coefficient on the baseball. I first wrote about the role of decreasing drag in boosting home runs in 2017, and MLB's commission of scientists and statisticians later confirmed that the more aerodynamic baseballs in use that year were largely to blame for the spike in home runs. The same commission rejected some alternate hypotheses, like rising temperatures and a league-wide boost in launch angle pushing more balls over the fence.

The current era has featured some large fluctuations in drag coefficient, leading to first an explosion in 2016 and 2017, and then a dialing back of homers last year. Curious about the record-breaking home run tallies in the last few days, I used the same methodology to measure the aerodynamics of the baseballs so far in 2019.

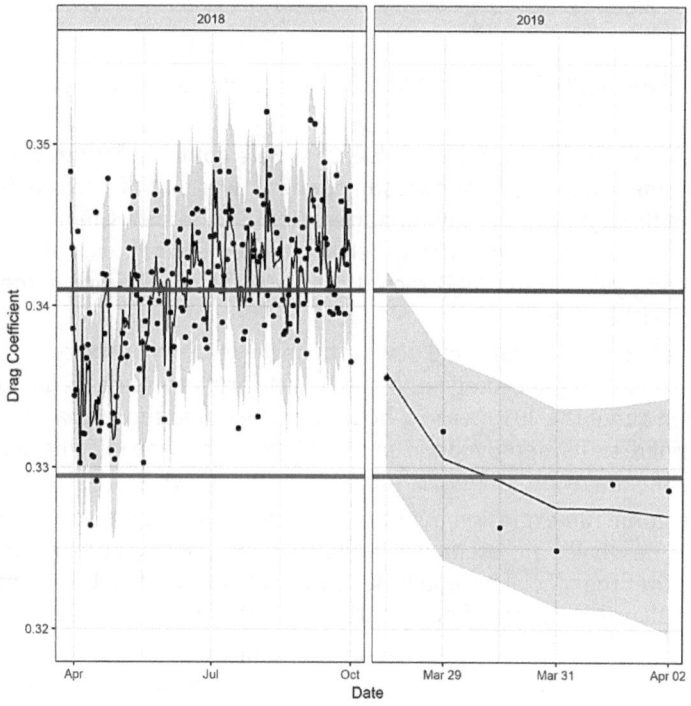

We're only a week into the 2019 season, but the drag numbers so far are among the lowest recorded in the last calendar year. With apologies for gory math, the current 2019 season average drag coefficient (the red line) would be below the 95 percent credible interval (the shaded area) for about nine-tenths of the 2018 season. (I used a Bayesian Random Walk model implemented in INLA to calculate these credible intervals, averaging the drag numbers in each game and adjusting for park.)

There were only a handful of six-day stretches in 2018 that had drag numbers below what we're seeing now, and most were in late June and early July. All of this means that 2019's data so far is quite a bit different than what we saw through most of last year.

These drag coefficients factor out the effects of temperature and air density, so they aren't a product of April cold. However, the numbers could be deceptive if the radars used to track pitches have changed from year to year. I consulted with some experts within baseball who were not aware of any specific modifications to the radar this year that could produce this pattern, but it's an important caveat of which to be aware.

On the one hand, it's only been six days, and we don't quite have the statistical basis to say that these drag coefficients are unprecedented compared to 2018. On the other hand, we've witnessed about 5,000 fastballs so far this season, so it's not as if our sample size is small. At least so far, the baseball has played like it's much more aerodynamic than it was last year. In fact, the current drag coefficient is really only comparable to 2017, when the baseballs were more aerodynamic than they had been in at least a decade.

It's not just fancy radar tracking indicating that the baseball is flying through the air more easily. The current number of home runs per game (as of this writing) is the highest it's been since the heady days of 2017, the year that teams and players broke dinger-related records everywhere you looked. That's especially remarkable considering that we're in what is typically the coldest part of the regular season, when lower temperatures and higher winds tend to suppress offense and keep balls in the air within the park. Comparing only from April to April, this year's rate of home runs per fly ball is even a little bit higher than it was in 2017.

With that said, the current measurements are no guarantee that 2019 will be another year of record-shattering homer hitting. The trouble with the drag measurements is that they are not consistent from June to August, from week to week, or even sometimes from day to day. Whether because of natural manufacturing variation or differences in the underlying supplies of cowhide and thread that go into the baseballs, drag has a tendency to fluctuate up and down over the course of a year. So the homers that fly in the first week of April wouldn't necessarily clear the fence a week later.

It's possible that this one-week drop in drag coefficient subsides and the baseball returns to its 2018 levels. On the other hand, it's almost equally probable that the ball becomes even more slippery and flies ever farther. Either way, it's clear that the baseball's air resistance is something to keep an eye on for the remainder of the 2019 season.

—*Robert Arthur is an author of Baseball Prospectus.*

The Moral Hazard of Playing It Safe

Craig Goldstein

This article originally appeared at Baseball Prospectus on August 6, 2019.

A couple days prior to the trade deadline, amidst a sea of tranquility posing as the lead up to the trade deadline, Bob Nightengale took to Twitter. Nightengale, who was probably wearing his pants backwards at the time, tweeted that MLB GMs were coming around on the idea that the unified trade deadline should be moved back from July 31 to August 15, so they could better assess their positions in the standings and whether they should buy or sell. To which I said:

This might strike some as reductive and churlish. And it might be that, but it isn't really wrong, either. Jeff Quinton wrote a great piece discussing the environmental factors that enable front offices to avoid risk without upsetting the apple cart within their own fanbases. I don't believe that it goes far enough, however. His article gives us the proper framework through which to understand why these behaviors have been allowed to seep into front offices throughout the league. Understanding the reasons behind these actions are different from excusing them, though, and GMs should not be let off the hook for their non-competitive approach to the trade deadline (much less the offseason).

⚾ ⚾ ⚾

It's fair to say that fans as a group have rarely, if ever, been pro-player. It is also fair to say that in the time during and following the Moneyball revolution, the pendulum swung from fans who cared intensely about winning in the moment (and thus might be intolerant of a rebuilding approach) to fans who supported building a team that could compete throughout multiple seasons, viewing the playoffs as a crapshoot, with the thought that getting multiple bites at the apple was a better approach than taking a bigger bite in any one season.

There's nothing wrong with that approach, and I still find merit in that argument. However, it seems that the pendulum has swung too far in that direction. Teams are overvaluing some of the individual factors that make themselves long-term contenders rather than attempting to seize a championship when given the opportunity. It's a difficult needle to thread.

And surely, they (and those in similar positions) would have liked another two weeks to clarify where they stand so as to better marshal their resources. We've all asked for a few more minutes when staring at a menu. But all of these GMs and front office personnel are where they are to make difficult decisions. They have proprietary data and internal analysts dedicated to understanding their position relative to the rest of the league, and how any move in the here and now impacts their long-term vision. To complain (if that report is accurate) that over half the season is not enough to properly assess their season is bullshit of the highest order. Move the deadline, and you'd simply have increasingly discounted trade offers because teams would be acquiring even less control of anyone they're acquiring, rental or not.

Major league front offices are behaving like the managers they lampooned two decades ago. They're effectively sacrificing a runner to second in the ninth inning—not because it's the correct move, but rather because it is safe. It used to be that the phrase "moral hazard" was used to describe general managers who made ill-fated, short-sighted decisions aimed at locking in wins and securing their jobs at the expense of their team's future. Now, general managers are guilty of committing moral hazards in the opposite direction, playing it utterly safe and terrified of becoming scapegoats.

In lieu of bold action, they opt to pussyfoot around a current window of contention, choosing instead to play the long game and stack up years of control like they're blocks in a game of Jenga. GMs pass on signing quality players in free agency because the back-end of the deal might look bad, and because they might be able to squeeze out 70 percent of the production from a player who costs a tenth as much. That's a safer investment, too, because it's also hard to prove a negative—it's impossible to prove that Manny Machado would make the Mets a playoff team in 2019-2020, but it's easy to say that the back half of Robinson Cano's contract sucks. Owners, who rule over GM's jobs, are also humans with human brain processes that will always make the so-called albatross contract uglier than the road not taken.

These days, GMs are remembered for the bad deals they make and the surplus value they generate, not the acquisition of expensive, necessary talents that meet their market worth (or fall slightly short while still providing significant on-field value). And front offices know that one or two expensive misfires can cost them their jobs, no matter how many good deals they make.

No front office exemplifies this ethos more than the Toronto Blue Jays. General Manager Ross Atkins had this to say following the Blue Jays underwhelming trade deadline:

This is by no means the first time that an executive will cite years of control to justify their actions, which is often just another way of saying "don't look at what we got, look at how much we got of it." Atkins touts quantity to elide the discussion of quality—either, that of the players acquired, or those given up. Remember: the other teams presumably value years of control, too.

Atkins also had some thoughts to offer regarding free agents back in early 2018:

This ignores, of course, whether the player can create enough value in the front end of a contract to justify the longer term of a deal, and the decline that often occurs in the back end. It also ignores whether the player can fill a need the team requires and put them in a position to compete for and win a championship. But as teams seemingly avoid contention at all, where they might end up having to consider and later justify some of these tough decisions, we still see risk-averse approaches.

Anthony Fenech's article on two trades that recently extended GM Al Avila didn't make got at this issue rather well:

> Passing on those deals was defensible: Both players had yet to break out and trading [Michael] Fulmer—a pitcher who appeared to be a future ace, no matter his injury concerns—would have taken serious gumption, opening Avila up to strong criticism.

Avoiding strong criticism is something each of us can understand as a motivation, but the avoidance of criticism only matters if that criticism is valid. In Fulmer's case, shoving his injury concerns aside affects not only the years that the team controls him (he is currently missing a full season due to Tommy John surgery) but also the quality of those seasons, as his knee and elbow injuries combined to dampen his effectiveness even when healthy enough to pitch. But it was easy to present the then-current image of Fulmer as a top of the rotation pitcher who the team had under its domain for the next five seasons as something to build around. The status quo isn't nearly as often second-guessed as a decision that disrupts it.

⚾ ⚾ ⚾

MLB GMs are risk-averse to a fault. They are ivy-educated and consulting firm-approved, and yet they can't seem to avoid leaving wins on the table in their all-consuming lust for a non-existent $/WAR championship. They are supposed to zig when everyone else zags, and not merely pay lip service to the idea of zigging through a calculated PR plan built on convincing the fan base their approach is novel when it actually apes most of their competitors. Instead they've become far more concerned with making safe, accepted-by-the-new-common-wisdom decisions, such that our prior understanding of what a moral hazard is has become inverted.

I can't blame them entirely, and not only because of the reasons that Quinton illuminated in his article, but also because of the damage wrought by the introduction of the second wild card (WC2) spot. MLB's desire to have more teams in playoff contention has sparked anti-competitive behavior. Teams know now that they do not need to swing big as they assemble their roster because there is a good chance that a mediocre team can either catch fire and capture a division, or muddle along until they back into the WC2.

Simultaneously, the one-game playoff has neutered the WC1, putting an entire season on the flip of a coin like some sort of baseball-obsessed Anton Chigurh. While the one-game playoff makes sense as a way to increase the value of winning a division, it also means that if a front office doesn't like its chances of overcoming a behemoth like the Dodgers or Astros in the offseason, they have few incentives to chase glory. Similarly, the relative inaction in the NL Central at the trade deadline—despite a wide open division—can be explained by the idea that any high-variance investment could still result in only a wild card (or worse) result, given the mere two months left in the season to make an impact.

⚾ ⚾ ⚾

As stated at the top, we should not confuse reasons for excuses. The implementation of the second wild card is just one of many environmental factors that influence how each front office operates. I am convinced that it is one of the larger factors, but I am also convinced that organizations need to shed the yoke of "efficiency at all costs" so that they can instead pursue competition, as the spirit of the game intends. Until they do, we're all deadline losers.

—*Craig Goldstein is an author of Baseball Prospectus.*

Index of Names

Abreu, José	20	Gonzalez, Gio	66
Adolfo, Micker	97, 112	Gonzalez, Luis	85, 111
Anderson, Tim	22	Grandal, Yasmani	34
Bañuelos, Manny	46	Guerrero, Tayron	68
Basabe, Luis Alexander	84, 107	Hamilton, Ian	94
Beard, James	97, 114	Hansen, Alec	99, 114
Bummer, Aaron	48	Herrera, Kelvin	70
Burdi, Zack	99	Heuer, Codi	99
Burr, Ryan	99	Jiménez, Eloy	36
Bush, Bryce	112	Johnson, Tyler	99
Cease, Dylan	50	Keuchel, Dallas	72
Cishek, Steve	52	Kopech, Michael	95, 105
Collins, Zack	24, 108	Lambert, Jimmy	96, 111
Colomé, Alex	54	López, Reynaldo	74
Cordero, Jimmy	56	Madrigal, Nick	86, 104
Cuthbert, Cheslor	26	Marshall, Evan	76
Dalquist, Andrew	110	Mazara, Nomar	38
Delmonico, Nicky	97	McCann, James	40
Despaigne, Odrisamer	58	Medeiros, Kodi	99
Detwiler, Ross	99	Mejía, Adalberto	78
Dunning, Dane	107	Mendick, Danny	42
Encarnación, Edwin	28	Mercedes, Yermin	97
Engel, Adam	30	Minaya, Juan	99
Escobar, Alcides	97	Moncada, Yoán	44
Flores Jr., Bernardo	93, 112	Palka, Daniel	87
Foster, Matt	99	Pilkington, Konnor	99, 113
Frare, Caleb	99	Reed, AJ	97
Fry, Jace	60	Robert, Luis	88, 103
Fulmer, Carson	62	Rodón, Carlos	80
García, Leury	32	Ruiz, José	82
Giolito, Lucas	64	Rutherford, Blake	89, 113

Sanchez, Yolbert 111
Santiago, Hector 99
Sheets, Gavin 90, 109
Skole, Matt 97
Sosa, Lenyn 109
Stiever, Jonathan 97, 106
Thompson, Matthew 110
Vaughn, Andrew 91, 106
Vieira, Thyago 99
Zavala, Seby 92